THE TIN KAZOO

TELEVISION, POLITICS, AND THE NEWS

Other Books by Edwin Diamond

The Science of Dreams
The Rise and Fall of the Space Age

Contributor to

The Five Worlds of Our Lives
The Media and the Cities
Our Troubled Press

THE TIN KAZOO: EDWIN D
POLITICS, TELEVISION, A

The MIT Press
Cambridge, Massachusetts, and London, England

AMOND THE TIN KAZOO:
D THE NEWS POLITICS, TE

This book was set in IBM Composer Press Roman
by Allen Wayne,
printed on Finch Title 93
by Murray Printing Company,
and bound in Columbia Milbank Linen MBL 4320
by Murray Printing Company
in the United States of America.

Library of Congress Cataloging in Publication Data

Diamond, Edwin.
    The tin kazoo.

    Bibliography: p.
    Includes index.
    1. Television broadcasting of news—United States.
I. Title.
PN4888.T4D5   384.55'4'0973   75-17905
ISBN 0-262-04048-4

CONTENTS

ACKNOWLEDGMENTS

This book grew out of an undergraduate lecture course that I first taught in the Department of Political Science at the Massachusetts Institute of Technology, Cambridge, beginning in the fall of 1971. To the officers, faculty, and students of the Institute go my thanks and appreciation, but particularly to Jerome Wiesner, Walter Rosenblith, Dr. Benson Snyder, Eugene Skolnikoff, Myron Weiner, and Ithiel de Sola Pool. I am also grateful to the Institute of Politics of the John F. Kennedy School of Government, Harvard University, where I led study groups in 1973 and 1974. Some of this material has appeared, in different form, in the *Columbia Journalism Review* and in *New York* magazine, and I am grateful for the help and guidance of Kenneth Pierce of *CJR* and Clay S. Felker and Sheldon Zalaznick of *New York*. The men and women in the newsroom of WTOP-TV of Washington, one of the Post-Newsweek Stations, Inc., were also extremely helpful. Larry Israel, Joel Chaseman, James Snyder, John Baker, and Terry Reynolds in particular were willing to share their knowledge and experience with someone from the "print press" (as Ron Ziegler used to call it). Al Primo and Av Westin of ABC News, Earl Ubell, Lee Hanna, and Richard Wald of NBC News, Richard Salant and Sanford Socolow of CBS News, and Paul Klein of Computer Television, Inc., were also patient teachers. And Loraine Bennett, Adelina Diamond, and Howard Webber were skilled editors. I alone am responsible for the judgments and conclusions here.

Finally, my deepest appreciation goes to the faculty and student members of the News Study Group in the Department of Political Science at MIT. Literally dozens of young men and women made contributions. The following require specific mention: John Kavazanjian, Raissa Deber, Debora Dehoyos, Daryl Desmond, Susan Eisner, John Hanzel, Michael McNamee, Barbara Moore, David Olive, Claude Owre, Richard Parker, Meg Power, Craig Reynolds, Norman Sandler, Paul E. Schindler, Peggy Seminario, and David Tenenbaum. This book is dedicated to them.

Sands Point, N.Y.   Edwin Diamond
May 1975

All that the sharpest critics of democracy have alleged is true, if there is no steady supply of trustworthy and relevant news. Incompetence and aimlessness, corruption and disloyalty, panic and ultimate disaster, must come to any people which is denied an assured access to the facts. No one can manage anything on pap. Neither can a people.

Walter Lippmann
Liberty and the News (1920)

I'm going to tell you a story and after I tell it, you will know all there is to know about television news. . . .The executives of this station [in New York] were watching all three news shows one night. There had been a fire in a Roman Catholic orphanage on Staten Island. One executive complained that a rival station had better film coverage. "Their flames are higher than ours," he said. But another executive countered: "Yes, but our nun is crying harder than theirs. . . ."

TV Reporter to Interviewer (1974)

INTRODUCTION

The day that memorial services were held at the Washington Cathedral for the journalist and commentator Walter Lippmann, who died in December 1974, the *Washington Post* devoted an editorial to Lippmann's contributions to the profession of journalism. As the editorial recalled, Lippmann was once accused by a colleague of "always dredging up basic principles. . . ." That won't do in daily journalism, the colleague explained, and offered this metaphor: a piano has eight octaves, a violin three, and a bugle only four notes. "Now if what you've got to play is a bugle," the friend concluded, "there isn't any sense in camping down in front of piano music."

"You may be right," Lippmann replied, "but I'm not going to spend my life writing bugle calls."

I considered entitling this book *Bugle Call Rag*, for it is my contention that most of the daily press in America, and particularly television journalism, has been satisfied to play only three or four notes as far as the public news is concerned. In the end, I concluded that "bugle" might be too imposing an instrument; *Tin Kazoo*, however, has the right sound (in 1964, John Schneider published a novel called *The Golden Kazoo*, which described the supposedly seductive tunes played by television advertising).

Many people, academics and politicians alike, profess to see in television and the "mass media" a potent instrument of political and social influence. In theory, they may be right. Television has enormous potential for

conveying emotions. The public dramas of our lives have
been played out on television: the riderless horse in the
funeral cortege of John F. Kennedy, the Reverend Martin
Luther King, Jr., speaking at Lincoln Memorial, the ghost-
ly figures of the first Apollo astronauts on the lunar surface. On these occasions, television carried the powerful
images into all our memories. But in the coverage of the
daily concerns of our polity—what I call the public news—
television has been an uncertain and weak instrument, a
tin kazoo. Television journalism has, in the main, hesi-
tated to deliver that "steady supply of trustworthy and
relevant news" that Walter Lippmann thought was necessary to a democracy. Too often television has been
content to take the easier path of irrelevant coverage:
sports, weather, traffic accidents, and smoky fires. Too
often, "access to the facts" has been translated to mean
higher flames and more tearful nuns.

The chapters that follow try to go back to some of the
basic principles of daily journalism. The first half of the
book (Part I) is descriptive; Chapters 1 through 5 are
concerned with the reach and pervasiveness of the television medium, with the television audience, and with
television forms—both for the local news and for network
news. Part II consists of a number of case studies of major political events of the 1960s and early 1970s, including the Indochina War, the Nixon presidency, the Watergate scandals, and the political campaigns of those years.
The examples discussed are not confined to television
journalism. From these specifics—for example, from such
"simple" matters as the name given the "enemy" in Indochina—I try to reach some general conclusions, appli-
cable to all the media.

A final word: I was urged to make some "recommendations for the future"—to set down what changes are needed in the practice of television journalism. There are some recommendations here, particularly at the end of the two chapters on the news forms (Chapters 4 and 5); but there is no program for action. It has been my experience in newsrooms around the country that most broadcast journalists know what must be done—or undone. They know, without being hectored, the need for more time, more money, more care, more thought—in a word, more professionalism—in order to improve the coverage of politics, government, and the public news.

Part I

NEWS FORMS
AND THE AUDIENCE

Chapter 1
The Tin Kazoo

While many politicians have relied on television to reach voters or influence public opinion during their careers, few public figures have put so much faith in the powers of the medium for so long a time as Richard Nixon. In 1952, he turned to television—his emotional Checkers speech—in a last, successful effort to stop the drive to remove him from the Republican national ticket as his party's vice-presidential candidate. In 1960, he agreed to the televised Kennedy-Nixon debates in the confidence—mistaken, it turned out—that he would easily show up his less experienced opponent. In the 1968 presidential campaign, he made such extensive use of controlled television appearances that the entire campaign was memorialized as a model of "the selling of the President." Finally, between 1969 and 1974, during the 2,027 days of his presidency, he summoned the network cameras to the White House Oval Office no fewer than 37 times in order to address the national television audience.

One of the most critical of these appearances came on Monday night, April 30, 1973, as the Watergate scandals and cover-up were beginning to come apart. In the past, television had helped Nixon explain his actions to the nation; on April 30, he plainly intended to use it again to rally support. Among the presidential decisions announced that night were the resignations of Mr. Nixon's closest assistants and his attorney general and the firing of his counsel, John W. Dean III. The President also announced that while he was taking overall responsibility for the whole

CHAPTER 1 . . . THE TIN KAZOO

Watergate matter, at the same time he claimed he was innocent of any wrongdoing in connection with the initial burglary and the subsequent cover-up efforts. Nixon explained that he had been occupied with the larger duties of his office, journeying to China and the Soviet Union, "winding down" the war in Indochina. As the President spoke from the Oval Office, the camera picked up the seal of the President of the United States. On one side of Nixon's desk was an American flag; visible in the background was a photograph of the Nixon family. The President was low-key; he looked right into the camera. He was direct, serious, "sincere." It was, after all, his first major public move to affect national opinion on Watergate in the nine months that the scandal had been growing. The stakes were high: an estimated 80 to 85 million Americans were watching the presidential broadcast, almost 75 percent of the total television audience in the United States.

All in all, it was a vintage Nixon performance. When he finished the broadcast, a television technician complimented him on the speech; the technician noted that there were tears in the President's eyes. Still restless and keyed up—like a horse after a race—Mr. Nixon went to the Press Room in the West Wing of the White House. There he told the startled reporters—they hadn't seen the President for a news conference in several weeks—to keep watching him closely and to continue to say he is wrong when he is wrong.

Then something else rather startling happened. In the week following the President's address, the public opinion analyst Louis Harris conducted a telephone poll of a national sampling of voters.[1] Harris's findings, relatively unremarked at the time, indicated that Mr. Nixon's "over-all job rating"—how well the public thought he was per-forming the functions of a president—had reached some-thing of a standoff: 48 percent of the sample felt "posi-tive" about him, and 48 percent said they felt "negative." Before the televised talk, the President's job rating had been 50 percent positive and 49 percent negative. Nixon's carefully crafted presentation, delivered before the mass of adult Americans, had not changed the balance in his favor at all. If anything, he had lost ground.

The currently accepted wisdom about television holds that it is a major key to political power. *Presidential Tele-vision,* a recent study sponsored by the Twentieth Cen-tury Fund, concluded that the ease of presidential access to the prime-time television audience, as exemplified by Nixon's 37 Oval Office appearances, had helped tip the balance of power in government away from the legisla-ture and the judiciary.[2] Similarly, implicit in the efforts by such groups as Common Cause to put limits on the amount of money that political candidates can spend is the idea that the public must be "protected" from slick media campaigns on television. Many election reform pro-posals, in fact, limit the amount of spending on television advertising a candidate is permitted, while putting no lim-its on print advertising or other campaign techniques.

In the past, it has been true that *any time* the President—*any* president—appears on television and states his case to 85 million Americans, his job ratings have gone up. The rise apparently occurs even when the President may be announcing bad tidings, for example, new price and wage controls or the latest incursion of American military power in Southeast Asia. The idea is that when the

President appears on television in his role of leader of all the people—the only President we have and, as Lyndon Johnson once admonished a television official, "the leader of the free world"—then several million viewers automatically rally to his side. The Nixon White House staff advisers in particular were strong believers in "presidential television." An unexpected insight into just how the Nixon apparatchiks regarded the American public in this respect was provided in documents released by the House Judiciary Committee as part of its impeachment investigations in July 1974. In a memorandum to H. R. "Bob" Haldeman, written in the summer of 1971, at the time of the publication of the Pentagon Papers, Charles Colson makes the following observations:

According to Lou Harris' theory (and Howard Smith's interestingly enough) at least 50 per cent of the American people at least will always believe what any President tells them because they want to believe what any President tells them. If the President goes on television and makes a flatout statement, people tend to want to believe it. . . . I question therefore, whether this incident [release of the Papers by Daniel Ellsberg] has caused any further erosion of Presidential credibility—maybe some but not a great deal—and there are ways we can rebuild President Nixon's credibility.

Many academic researchers have gone along with this rather low view of public opinion formation. For example, Michael J. Robinson and Philip M. Burgess of Ohio State University studied a sampling of Columbus, Ohio, viewers after Senator Edward M. Kennedy's Chappaquiddick speech in July 1969; they concluded that the Senator improved his "image" with viewers as a result of his televised "explanation" of the drowning accident.[3] Robinson and Burgess argue that one-sided or "directed" information—

communication, such as the Checkers and Chappaquiddick speeches, not followed by any commentary that con-
tradicts the facts or criticizes the performance—can significantly modify public opinion.

Some vestiges of the "commander-in-chief effect" and
the "directed communications effect" were, of course,
evident after Richard Nixon's April 30 Watergate speech.
Most people polled, Harris reported, thought the televised appearance did more good than harm; by a vote of
51 to 37 percent, the majority felt that "the President
has gone a long way toward restoring public confidence
in the integrity of the White House." Yet, overall, the
presidential television appearance had resulted in some
personal slippage for Mr. Nixon. While the slippage
seemed to be small, it was a political blow of major pro-
portions, for his ratings should have gone up.

What happened? It might be argued, first of all, that
since President Nixon was appearing in a *party* role,
rather than talking about foreign or military policy, the
commander-in-chief effect was, as they used to say in the
Nixon White House, inoperative. But in past partisan appearances, notably the Checkers speech of 1952,
Mr. Nixon had done exceedingly well using television to
get his message across. After Checkers, there were also
tears in Richard Nixon's eyes—as well as an outpouring
of telegrams and cards. (Nixon had asked that viewers
write to keep his candidacy alive; they did so, in impressive numbers, and whatever Dwight Eisenhower's private
wishes about his running mate, Nixon remained on the
ticket.)

Second, it could be argued that, since the Watergate
mess was so rank, no amount of television aerosol—even

one complete with flag and family—could effectively de-odorize it. The public threshold of nausea, however, has, in the past, always been extremely high. John F. Kennedy achieved his best standings in the Harris and Gallup popularity polls *after* the incredibly botched Bay of Pigs invasion in 1961. For months after the Watergate scandal had surfaced, too, a large majority of the voters continued to tell the Harris polltakers they believed that both political parties engaged in political dirty tricks: Watergate was "no big deal."

There is, of course, a third possibility, one that has grown all but unthinkable over the last twenty years. It just may be that television is no longer as potent a political tool as the textbook wisdom holds. Or, to put the same heretical thought in another way, it may be that the audience—the political consumer—of the 1970s has changed in some critical ways. Perhaps what worked with the audience for Checkers in 1952 and with the audience for the Bay of Pigs in 1961 could no longer work for Watergate in 1973. Perhaps television, this great instrument of persuasion—the "Golden Kazoo" so coveted by politicians and admen—has become blunted and tinny by overuse or misuse. Perhaps viewers are simply smarter, more sophisticated, or more skeptical.

This is an extraordinarily difficult question to answer. The ambiguous response to the April 30 speech, by itself, proves little. But there have been other signs that some changes have taken place in public attitudes toward politics and political leadership, as well as in the political use of television.

Mr. Nixon made a second televised Watergate address on August 15, 1973; he repeated his contention that he "had no prior knowledge of the Watergate break-in" and had not taken part in the cover-up. According to a Gallup poll commissioned by the *New York Times*, about 44 percent of the people who watched the address on television found the speech "not at all" convincing, while 27 percent concluded it was "completely" convincing or "quite a lot." The survey was conducted by telephone the next night from a national sample of 810 adults. The poll also showed that 77 percent of those questioned saw the Nixon address on television, an unusually high figure that indicated a strong interest in the subject. Gallup also reported that half of those who watched the address did not believe the President's statement that he had no involvement in the planning or cover-up of the Watergate burglary, that 56 percent believed that he should turn over the tape recordings of his meetings with aides to the Senate Watergate Committee and to the courts, and that 58 percent disagreed with the President's statement that civil rights demonstrations, antiwar protests, and a "wave" of "terrorist" bombings had helped create the atmosphere that led to the Watergate crimes. So much for the Colson theory.

The unexpected responses to the two Nixon addresses are not the only recent evidence that some shift has taken place in public attitudes. There are other, equally important signs in television viewing habits, in voting patterns, and—significantly—in the behavior of the political candidates themselves. Roland Cole, a Harvard graduate student, made a survey of the campaign expenditures of all the major party U.S. Senate candidates in 1972—when there was a special limit, by act of Congress, of six cents per voter on broadcast advertising for candidates for federal office, but no ceilings at all on print advertising or expenditures for other campaign techniques.[4] Among other things, Cole found that

—Not many candidates reached the special limits put on media spending in 1972, and those who did simply decided to spend more on direct mail or other nonlimited activities.

—A candidate's percentage of the final vote tended to be very closely related to his percentage of total spending in that race. Winners thus generally spent more than losers, but winners and losers did not spend significantly different amounts per vote received.

—More dollars went for TV and radio than any other single activity, but these expenditures still averaged less than 20 percent of total spending, and they seemed to be reaching saturation levels in many states. On the basis of the 1972 patterns, other types of spending, such as direct mail or voter canvassing, appear far more likely to rise in coming years.

—When a victorious challenger outspent his incumbent opponent, the money didn't go on TV and advertising but rather on staff, telephones, campaign materials, and special events—items that usually mean a strategy emphasizing free media coverage and heavy voter canvassing.

"The losing incumbent is perhaps not the conscientious, close-to-his-district Senator swept aside by raw money and a media blitz," Cole suggests, "but the Senator who has drifted away from his district. . . ."

The election of 1972, perhaps, was an idiosyncratic one. But, then, aren't most elections? The fact that many candidates didn't bother to spend right up to the ceiling of their allowable broadcast advertising dollars suggests at least that a fresh look ought to be taken at some of the "axioms" of media politics, and at some of the rest of the accepted wisdom about television.

Chapter 2
Television: Less than Meets the Eye?

Few people are very far from a television set in the United States, which is a major reason why someone with something to sell—an advertising agency, say, or a political candidate—has such high regard for the medium. By the mid-1970s, some 97 percent of all American homes had at least one television set; almost one in every three households had two or more sets. One in ten households had *three* or more sets. And in those places where television so far hasn't, for social or technical reasons, been able to reach—cars, large offices, boats, cabins in vacation areas—radio has penetrated. Some 131 million Americans (83 percent of the population over the age of twelve) listened to radio on an April day in 1973 when polltakers called.

The fact that there are more television sets in the United States than telephones, bathtubs, or toilets no longer surprises most people.[1] More remarkably, perhaps, the average household set in 1973 was turned on about six hours a day—closer to seven hours in the winter months. Each year through the early 1970s, in fact, the "typical" set was staying on about 14 minutes more per day over the course of a year. Although some strong-eyed people may have watched all six hours, the average amount of viewing per person per day was about 2 hours and 45 minutes in 1973. The TV set, on the average, flickered more for women than for men, more for people over fifty than for those under fifty, more for blacks than for whites, more for the poor than for the rich, and more for the grade-school-educated than for the college-educated—but not much more. The latter point is important; a variety of surveys have purported to show that the educated and well-to-do don't watch much television. But when the figures for daytime viewing are averaged out and the audience after 6:00 P.M. only is measured—in order to create what Dr. Robert Bower, of the Bureau of Social Science Research, Washington, D.C., calls the "equal opportunity audience"—there isn't that much difference in the amount of viewing on the average that *any* population group does. The better-educated viewer, the evening figures indicated, watched as much as the poorly educated viewer, although the educated viewer may *claim* to watch less—because of feelings, the askers of such surveys believe, that "intellectuals" are supposed to look down their noses at television and are supposed to have a strong loyalty to "print culture."

For both college graduate and hard hat, then, television watching had become in the 1970s the most frequent human activity after sleep and ahead of working, eating, or making love. In fact, when Bower studied the evening habits of some 344 ordinary men and women in Minneapolis–St. Paul in 1970, he found that two out of every three people were watching television on an ordinary night in late winter.[2] So many people were watching that Bower became curious about what those few *other* people did instead of watching television the evening before. He found the pattern of behavior shown in the table (p. 15).

Minneapolis–St. Paul is a modest-sized city, Middle American yet urban. It is not New York City, but no one before has suggested that they roll up the sidewalks or sound "lights out" at 8:00 P.M. *Time* magazine not so long ago singled out the Twin Cities and Minnesota as the place where the Good Life still survives in America, a place

THE PEOPLE MACHINE . . .WHY PE

Television Survey, Minneapolis–St. Paul, 1970

"Did you watch any television yesterday evening after 6 P.M.? What were you doing instead of watching TV last night?"

Response	Percent
Yes, viewing television	65
No, outside the home—working	6
No, outside the home—shopping, visiting, out for dinner, church, etc.	16
No, doing chores inside the house (painting, cleaning, etc.)	4
No, other relaxing activity in the home (listening to radio, hi-fi, reading, hobbies, etc.)	8
No, other reasons, NA	1

Base: 100 percent = 344

Source: Robert T. Bower, *Television and the Public.*

of courtesy, culture, and unparalleled recreational facilities. Yet Bower calculates that if those citizens at work (6 percent) and those involved in necessary outside or inside chores (20 percent) are eliminated as potential viewers, then "we are left with only 8 or 9 per cent who had the opportunity but rejected television in favor of some other domestic leisure time pursuit for a whole evening." Some of his argument is a bit shaky, since the shoppers and the diners in a sense had the opportunity and rejected televiewing. If we accept his premise in part, however, his conclusion is unavoidable, even for the Good Life state of Minnesota: in a sample of average Americans, "there is not much going on at home for most people that can vie with the attractions of television." Bower found a few

WATCH . . . THE NIELSEN NUMBE

readers, a few music lovers, even a few who said they "just sat around. . . ." But these nonwatchers added up to a very small group who were not busy and still deliberately chose to do something else.

The Minneapolis–St. Paul figures agree with most of the research into the television audience, including the ratings figures of the A. C. Nielsen Company. On any late winter–early spring evening, between 60 and 66 percent of the 62 million television households in the United States (as of mid-1974) have the sets on. Since the number of viewers per household is about 2.2 in the evening hours, this means a total audience of 75 million is watching television nightly.

The People Machine

It is not hard to be impressed by these numbers. Robert MacNeil, the television correspondent, sought to describe the political muscle of television with the phrase in the title of his book, *The People Machine*.[3] The critic Robert Lewis Shayon has called television the great "crowd catcher." And the Reverend Everett Parker, head of the Office of Communication of the United Church of Christ and a leading advocate of broadening the base of television ownership, once wrote that television's "potential" for the "control of human beings and of nations" is perhaps greater than the threat—are you ready?—"of the atomic bomb or any weapon yet devised."

An audience of 75 million people has more than enough buying power to lift a product from obscurity and more than enough votes to elect a president. The metaphor of television as a great machine to collect people and transmit information is, seemingly, sustained by the statistics

RS . . .WHAT THE WAD WANTS . . .

of viewing. But it is much easier to count noses than to read minds. When the claims for television's "power" are examined critically, it may be that there is less than meets the eye in the great "people machine." The fact that vast numbers watch television night after night tells little about their reasons for watching, the level of their expectations, the content of the messages conveyed, and the degree of change—if any—that may take place in attitudes and behavior as a result of viewing. It is necessary to look into what brings viewers to the set in the first place, what is happening on the screen, and what the viewers take away from the set.

Why People Watch

One way to find out about an individual's personal habits and political attitudes is to ask him or her. But even this straightforward approach presents problems. People have quirky minds; a public opinion poll can be constructed with care in order to get a scientific sample of attitudes—only to be undermined by a kind of protective amnesia. Thus a canvass of voters' choices after an election often produces two results: more people claim to have voted in the elections than the totals show, and more people claim to have voted for the winner than his actual winning percentage shows. People tend to prevaricate, that is, to lie, to researcher-questioners. Usually the lies are told in an attempt to give the "right" (translation: respectable) response.

People also have the notorious ability to hold vastly different and clashing beliefs, attitudes, and ideas. We all know such people: hawks who opposed the Vietnam War, doves in favor of arms for Israel, working-class whites who may be against civil rights legislation but are friendly to blacks on the job, voters who told Gallup interviewers they were convinced Mr. Nixon wasn't telling the truth about his role in Watergate but at the same time didn't want him removed from office.

Recognizing, then, that the record of what people say they do may be an imperfect reflection of reality, one may nevertheless take it as a starting point. Two surveys of public attitudes toward television in particular are illuminating because they asked similar questions at critical points in the evolution of television. The studies are Gary Steiner's *The People Look at Television* and Bower's *Television and the Public*, mentioned above. Steiner's research was done in 1960, Bower's in 1970. Both studies used a standard survey research approach, interviewing a national cross section of the adult population. Steiner also included interviews with a smaller sample of New York City viewers. Ten years later, Bower asked many of the same questions, using interviewers from the Roper organization, which had helped out in 1960; for his close-up interviews, he chose Minneapolis–St. Paul instead of New York. Both studies were also sponsored by the Columbia Broadcasting System; there is no evidence that this sponsorship in any way influenced either Steiner's or Bower's results.

The people interviewed reported all sorts of specific positive feelings about television. In 1970, as in 1960, about half of all viewers said they watched television quite simply because television is "such a pleasant way to spend an evening." The most frequently cited reason offered in both 1960 and 1970 was "To see a specific program I enjoy very much." Other major reasons offered for watching were "To see a special program I've heard about," "Because I feel like watching television," "Because I think I

R TO APPLIANCE . . .THE AWAREN

can learn something" (offered more by the grade-school-
educated than by the college-educated viewer). Somewhat
less often cited as reasons for watching were "Because my
husband (or wife) is or seems to be interested," "Because
there is nothing else to do at the time," "To get away
from the ordinary cares and problems of the day," "Mainly to be sociable when others are watching," "Because I'm
afraid I might be missing something good."

The 1970 viewer also gave television highly positive
marks when compared to radio, newspapers, and magazines. Television was rated the medium that was

Most entertaining
Most educational
Most complete in news coverage
Most interest-creating
Most politically informative
Most public-spirited
Fairest and least biased
Most important personally

A key question in the 1960 survey, repeated in 1970,
listed five different "products and services designed to
please the general public." The five were automobiles,
television programs, fashions for women, popular music,
and movies. The samples were asked, "With which of
these five things are you personally most satisfied?" Television was the first choice of 29 percent of the audience
in 1960; by 1970 those satisfied with television had
dropped to 16 percent—even though public satisfaction
had increased for all the other categories. Automobiles,
for example, pleased almost half (48 percent) of Steiner's
public in 1960 and exactly half of Bower's in 1970. Asking somewhat the same question about television another

)F PROCESS

way, Bower found that the number of people who thought television was "getting worse all the time" had *almost doubled* in the last ten years—the same period in which watching had increased by an average of 50 minutes per household per day. People were watching more and more each year while claiming to enjoy their watching less and less.

The Nielsen Numbers

The extent of expressed public disenchantment with television is no longer news. While public respect for most American institutions has been falling in recent years, the drop-off for the mass media has been particularly severe. Two Louis Harris surveys, one taken in 1966, the other in 1971, reported that public esteem and confidence in television dropped so rapidly in that five-year period that only labor officials ranked below "television, the press and advertising" (Harris's grouping). Two years later, the press's role in exposing some of the Nixon Administration scandals had helped restore some public confidence, but the Watergate effect soon started wearing off.

What *is* news is that people, growing ever more disenchanted, still continue to watch more and more television. It may be that television has become, in people's minds, another utility like the telephone. People use the telephone because "it's there." It is useful, convenient, and it gets things done (most of the time), whatever anyone's feelings may be about the Telephone Company. But television, obviously, isn't a necessity in the same sense that the telephone is; if the viewers need television, it must be in some special way.

The Nielsen Television Index (NTI), the well-known
Nielsen rating numbers, is a second source of information
about viewer habits. The NTI is based not on what people
say but on what they do, specifically, on the recordings
made by audimeters—tiny electrical devices that connect
television sets to special telephone lines—installed in some
1,200 households across the United States to achieve a
random sample of viewers. Every 30 seconds around the
clock, the audimeter registers the channel that a set is
tuned to and transmits that reading in order to produce
the rating, which is nothing more or less than an audience
estimate, the circulation of a given program. In addition
to this metered sample, Nielsen and the American Research
Bureau (Arbitron) also have contracted with selected
households to keep viewing diaries in order to produce
local ratings in hundreds of metropolitan markets. Over
750,000 such diaries are tabulated annually. These rating
services are carefully audited; the networks, after all, pay
over $1 million a year for the privilege of reading the mea-
surements (advertising agencies pay less). There is little
reason to doubt their accuracy as *estimates;* network programming decisions involving hundreds of millions of dollars a year often ride on these numbers.

The Nielsen and the Arbitron ratings appear to disclose
another side of audience behavior: viewers watching television—as television—apparently independent of the content of the program watched. "The single most important
thing to know about the American television audience,"
says Paul Klein, for years the chief of audience research
at NBC in New York, "is its amazingly constant size."[4]
At any given moment, in the evening prime-time viewing

hours, there are about 36 million sets on *whether the network shows at that hour are strong, weak, so-so, or one of each.* Of course, the same person in each television household isn't watching through the evening, nor are the same 36 million households involved each night; the precise composition of the audience changes every half hour, but the overall number remains remarkably constant.

Underlying this consistency is television's version of Newton's law of inertia: a dial set at one station will remain at rest there unless acted upon by a strong force. Thus network programmers speak of *audience flow, lead-ins, lead-outs, hammocking,* and *Least Objectionable Programming.* Every August or so, ABC, CBS, and NBC begin a full advertising campaign during station breaks aimed at persuading viewers to set their dials to a network for the evening ("The best is right here. . ."). Television viewers are conceived of as a great river that grows throughout the day. Children, older people, and housewives control the dial during the day; as evening approaches, they are joined by working fathers or mothers at 5:00, 5:30, and 6:00 P.M. This audience continues to grow in the primetime hours (7:30–11:00 EST) and to flow in certain channels until it is diverted (by father, say, taking over the dial). A strong lead-in, then, is a program that delivers most of its audience to the program following it; in Boston, for example, the Channel 7 news increased its circulation dramatically after station management made "Candlepins for Cash," a game show, the lead-in. A strong lead-out is a program so popular that the audience tunes to its channel well before it begins; the late news on NBC stations across the country has done well traditionally because of the enduring popularity of the Johnny Carson "Tonight Show" that follows.

To hammock is to place a program—usually a new one—between two established, high-circulation winners to get both lead-in and lead-out bolstering effects. When CBS introduced a new comedy program called "Friends and Lovers" in 1974, the programmers hammocked it (think of a real hammock) between the enormously successful "All in the Family" and the equally popular "Mary Tyler Moore Show."

These terms are based upon an underlying assumption about the audience, the principle of the Least Objectionable Program. LOP—the idea is Paul Klein's—states that since people watch *television* rather than *particular programs,* they will choose, from among the three or four or five programs offered at any given time, the one "that can be endured with the least amount of pain and suffering." A good example of LOP in action has been the success of the ABC television program "Marcus Welby, M.D.," which was the ratings leader among all television programs in 1970–1971. During that television season, when "Marcus Welby" was achieving its highest Nielsen number on ABC, the rival network CBS was offering "60 Minutes," an excellent public affairs program done in "magazine" style, while NBC was offering "First Tuesday," also a public affairs program. In *New York* magazine, Klein explained how LOP dictates what people watch:

When asked what we want to see more of on TV, we keep on offering "news," "public affairs," or some other dignified, self-flattering response. *Marcus Welby*'s immense popularity shows that while we all say we want more public-affairs programming, we never said we wanted to view it (unless, of course, that is *all* there is to view). On Tuesday at 10 p.m. each week, CBS has either *60 Minutes* or some other terribly worthy public-affairs offering. This competition alone is enough to give *Welby* a respectable share of the available audience. But on the first Tuesday of each month NBC plays *First Tuesday,* no less worthy than *60 Minutes* and 60 minutes longer. On the first Tuesday of each month, then, *Welby* becomes the powerhouse. . . . Well over two-thirds of all homes viewing the networks at 10 to 11 p.m. decide that *Welby* is the LOP.

"And who can blame them?" Klein concludes. When a woman has syphilis on "Welby," we can expect a happy ending. When the same woman has it on "First Tuesday," we expect to catch it.

The audience flow figures suggest not only that people prefer to watch something rather than nothing—all the while, of course, feeling guilty about it—but that they may even prefer to watch nothing on television to doing something else, like reading or talking with their friends, spouses, or families. This is the reductio ad absurdum that can be drawn from the night of the Great Television Blackout of 1971 in New York City. On that Sunday night, February 7, 1971, a power failure occurring on the East Side of Manhattan temporarily knocked out the Empire State Building transmitter used by all the stations on the New York VHF television band. Elsewhere in the New York area electric power was normal—which meant that television sets still functioned, though with blank, sound-less screens. Nevertheless, according to the Nielsen audimeters, about a half-million New Yorkers continued to watch the blank screen—or at least left their sets on. "Nielsen's N.Y. overnight audimeter sample has some real video buffs," the newspaper *Variety* observed sardonically in a brief note the next week.

The image of the television viewer that comes through from audience flow theory is an all-too-familiar one: a mass audience, largely inert, near addicts of the tube. The audience has been described, in *Variety*'s words, as "video buffs," or as the "numbers" when advertisers count them, or as "Harriet Housewife" and "the mice" (children) in the conversations of the television programmers, with their hands over the microphone. A rural viewer is "Uncle Fud from Fudsville." His city cousin is "Joe Six Pack," the quintessential hard-hat, hard-core television viewer. Joe comes home at 5:00 P.M., perhaps earlier, washes up, eats, goes to the refrigerator for his six pack of beer, walks into the den, or "family room," turns on the set, and plops down in his favorite chair, not unlike Archie Bunker, the blue-collar hero of "All in the Family." If Joe's favorite channel has been programmed according to LOP, he isn't supposed to move again for hours, except to get another six pack when he has gone through the first six cans.

One of the most successful advertising campaigns in years, a network executive explained to me not so long ago, was the series of television commercials for the Schaefer Brewing Company. The key line in the commercials went: "Schaefer's is the one beer to have when you're having more than one. . . ." The ad agency, the executive explained, wasn't interested in winning over the occasional beer drinker who "buys a few bottles of beer when he stops in the supermarket and keeps them in the refrigerator for a week or so"; rather, it wanted "Joe Six Pack," who picks up six or twelve cans each night, who has more than one when he is drinking beer.

What the Wad Wants

Joe—and his family—are caricatures; but often exaggerated pictures take on a life of their own. Norman Mailer has elevated Joe into a collective political force, which he calls the "Wad." The television audience—the Wad—will watch the Least Objectionable Programming and actually be soothed by it. In *St. George and the God Father,* Mailer's report on the Democratic and Republican conventions of 1972, he expresses his grudging admiration (one pro to another pro) for the carefully scripted parade of nonevents leading to Nixon's renomination.[5] Script is the operative word, for Mailer saw the Nixon of 1972 as a political genius, a film director of sorts—"the Eisenstein of the mediocre and the inert"—who understands what the Wad want, and knows how to give it to them. The people who sit for hours in front of their TV sets, Mailer says, must use it as a kind of "videotronic tranquillizer." Nixon knows this and programs for all mass tastes. Mailer calls the Nixon approach "the Jeannette Weiss Principle" (after a singer at the convention's Sunday worship service); the idea is that "whenever possible use a black lady with a German Jewish name doing a patriotic bit." Thus Ray Bloch, the music director of the Convention Orchestra, had a name which at once might please Jews and Germans as he played music which satisfied every taste, running from Dixieland through Lawrence Welk to Lombardo.

This is vintage Mailer. But, for all the dazzle, the basic idea is shopworn: intellectuals have made the easy case that television is "the opiate of the masses" since the days of nine-inch black-and-white receivers. The Wad, narcotized, dumbly following the programming directions set for it, may have been a fairly accurate concept for a time when television was new, but even that possibility is somewhat debatable. Lately, however, it has become increasingly inadequate as an explanation for viewer behavior. If the

Wad has not dissolved completely, then certainly its ranks have been thinned.

The evidence for this assumption comes from a variety of sources. Audience surveys show that the percentage of people who search around the dial for specific programs has increased in recent years. This selective viewer can't be dismissed as someone who merely gives researchers the "right" answers. He (and she) exists in the ratings books as well, particularly in the ratings for the news programs that often go on at the same early evening hours. The graphs for these news ratings have more and more come to resemble a fever chart as thousands and thousands of viewers make individual decisions to change their viewing preferences (see pp. 28–29). For example, millions of viewers in New York, Chicago, and Los Angeles jumped channels between 1971 and 1973 in order to tune in on the bright and informative "Eyewitness News" programs of ABC's local stations. In New York, between 1966 and 1973, the ratings curve of WNBC went straight down, while WABC gained steadily and WCBS remained fairly even. While the dial switching might be explained by the principle of LOP, many critics would argue that WABC's "Eyewitness News" was the best of the three competing news programs in terms of writing, film, graphics, and similar editorial values. In Boston, Channel 7's news may have benefited from its popular game show lead-in, but it also improved its news format considerably in the period of its circulation gains.

Among entertainment programs, too, quality in writing, direction, and performance has not, in recent years, been a hindrance to Nielsen success. "All in the Family," the comedy that in 1972 had replaced "Marcus Welby" as the

The Changing Audience for News

The two graphs are for the Washington, D.C., metropolitan area. The first shows the changing share of the audience for news achieved by the three competing news programs in the early evening hours; the second shows how this audience has grown in Washington over the last three years.

Early News Block: Washington

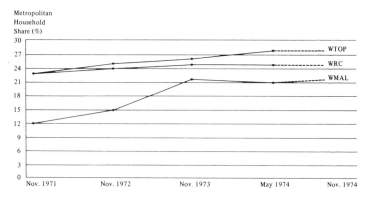

News Viewing in Washington

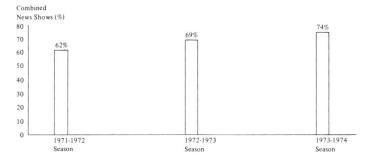

This chart shows the average share of viewing households watching news programming Monday–Friday, 6:00–7:30 P.M. (May, February–March, and November surveys of each season equal average).

In the fall of 1971, WMAL-TV expanded its local news. Thus all three network affiliates carry news programming from 6:00 to 7:30 P.M. (Monday–Friday) with one hour for local news and 30 minutes for network news. Local portions of WTOP and WMAL run from 6:00 to 7:00 P.M. with network news from 7:00 to 7:30. Until early 1975, WRC's local news ran from 6:00 to 6:30 and from 7:00 to 7:30 with network news from 6:30 to 7:00 P.M.

The share of those viewing households that are watching news from 6:00 to 7:30 at three points in each season:

	November	*February–March*	*May*
1973–1974	73%	75%	74%
1972–1973	64%	69%	75%
1971–1972	58%	59%	69%

Source: Nielsen Sample Index, courtesy Teddy Reynolds.

television series with the largest weekly audience, was considered by professional film writers to be the best-written series on television. "Maude" and "Sanford and Son," two other major ratings successes of 1973 and 1974 produced by the same people responsible for "All in the Family," were also professionally superior products of their kind. The same was true of the "Mary Tyler Moore Show" and one of its spin-offs, "Rhoda."

Television's commercials are often a sensitive gauge of which way the wind is blowing in these matters (advertisers sniff out trends quickly). In June 1974, a *New York Times* report confirmed what television viewers could not help but notice over the years: "real people"—nonprofessional men and women—were increasingly displacing actors in commercial spots. According to the *Times,*

Back in the early days of television, advertisers hired only models, beautiful people, to sell their products on the home screen. Later on in the fifties, personality/salesmen like Arthur Godfrey were in great demand. The sixties were the heyday of the character actor who looked like everybody's neighbor. Now, more and more companies that advertise on TV are looking for "real people" to do their selling for them. The buyers have, in effect, become the salesmen.

One of the admen interviewed in the *Times* article, John S. Bowen, president of Benton and Bowles, suggested that growing consumer skepticism of advertising claims had forced companies to use "real people." The trend was, said Bowen, "one way certain advertisers are dealing with the problem of getting consumers to believe them. They go to the people themselves and let them talk about their experience with the product. It's the advertiser saying, in effect, 'Don't take our word for it. Listen to what the actual user of the product has to say.' "

Perhaps the sharpest blow to the myth of video-tranquilized viewers came during the televised coverage of the Senate Watergate hearings. According to the national Nielsen ratings of mid-July 1973, the hearings consistently outdrew the normal daytime schedule of soap operas and game shows. Granted, the Watergate hearings were an exceptional news event, as well as compelling television drama ("Remarkable, unlikely cast of characters and script," *Variety* noted in a mock review). On the other hand, most of the daytime rating leaders bested by the hearings—shows like "Let's Make a Deal," "Split Second," "Newlywed Game," and "As the World Turns"—had been around for years, building loyal audiences ("As the World Turns" first went on the air in 1956). If there ever has been a Wad, it certainly would be the daytime television audience. Yet the audience figures for the Watergate hearings indicated that while hundreds of thousands of normally nondaytime viewers tuned in, as many, if not more, regular viewers switched over to the hearings. By the mid-1970s, as a matter of fact, even hammocks with the strongest rating supports were collapsing. In January 1975, CBS's "Friends and Lovers," hammocked between "All in the Family" and the "Mary Tyler Moore Show," sagged so much (at least as judged by CBS programmers) that it was taken off the air. A spin-off from "All in the Family" was put in its place.

As the picture of the audience-as-Wad dissolves, a number of other elements come into clearer focus. The reports, like Robert Bower's, of growing dissatisfaction with television are consistent with an audience that has become more demanding, or at least less dazzled; the rating successes of certain programs—public affairs offerings like the

CBS News "60 Minutes," entertainment shows like "The Waltons" (which was called "so natural . . . you have to worry about its survival" by the critic of *Chicago Today* when it first appeared in 1972)—are consistent with an audience that has become more selective; the fact that presidential speeches no longer produce automatic "rally-round-the-flag responses" is consistent with an audience that has become more sophisticated, or harder to manipulate.

It also becomes clearer that real understanding of television and its audiences is possible when they are approached dynamically rather than as static, frozen entities. Like any other institution in society, the institution of television grows and changes. The medium and its audience of the infant year of 1953 had changed by 1963; by 1973, medium and audience had both developed and were in a new relationship. The dates, obviously, are arbitrary, though some ten-year cycle—in programming, in the gestalt of the commercials, in viewer attitudes—appears to be operating.

Cycles of Television: From Wonder to Appliance
Consider what might be called the television of the fifties.[6] In the early 1950s, television sets were still relatively expensive. In 1949, an RCA 16-inch black-and-white set cost $469.50, and some 4 million homes had one (10 percent of all homes). The audience was mainly middle class and better educated; the opportunities of a new medium produced a sense of excitement and experimentation. A new technology was at hand. Performers like Dave Garroway and Ernie Kovacs developed a new informal style for television. Sid Caesar, Imogene Coca, Howard

Morris, and Carl Reiner made use of close-up cameras and
editing techniques to create superb comedy skits—many
of them satirizing films and television—on "Your Show of
Shows." "Playhouse 90" offered the plays of Paddy
Chayefsky, Tad Mosel, and other mature dramatists. The
CBS News team of Edward R. Murrow and Fred W.
Friendly produced a series of remarkable documentary
reports (which the CBS network has been rebroadcasting,
twenty years later, in its summertime "CBS News Retro-
spective" series). It wasn't the Golden Age of television,
as the nostalgists would have it. The wail of sirens and the
beat of hoofs heralded a hundred gone and best-forgotten
police dramas and horse Westerns—"Dragnet," "Big Town,"
"Highway Patrol," "Racket Squad," "The Line-up,"
"Cisco Kid," "Cheyenne," "Death Valley Days," "Fron-
tier," "Gunsmoke," "Tales of the Texas Ranger," ad
nauseam. Even the "hard-hitting" Murrow-Friendly reports often seem punchless in retrospect; when their 1954
report on national resources was rerun in July 1974, the
absence of any environmental spokesmen—and the attention given to industry leaders—jarred the consumerist
viewer of the seventies. Still, 1950s television was "new
and wonderful"; people reacted to it warmly, whole families viewing it together and telling researchers, such as
Gary Steiner, that they watched television because "it's a
pleasant way to spend an evening."

By the end of the 1950s, 46 million homes (88 percent
of all households) had at least one set, and the price of an
RCA 21-inch black-and-white receiver was $209. Televi-
sion had become a mass medium; only the very intellectual, and the very poor, didn't own one receiver. By
1960, too, its audience had been exposed to the quiz

show scandals. Charles Van Doren, the most famous of
the quiz show winners on the leading show, "Twenty-
One," confessed before a House of Representatives sub-
committee in early November 1959 that the questions
were rigged. He told how a producer had primed him
with answers to the questions he would be asked; the producer had explained that "the show was merely entertainment and giving help to the quiz contestants . . . was a
common practice and merely a part of show business."

It was an appropriate introduction to the television of
the 1960s. By 1963, the "penetration" (as the industry
sales people called it) of television into every home was
just about complete. The Wad had formed. Programming
was ruled by Nielsen and Arbitron numbers. For a variety
of reasons, mostly technical, small-town and rural viewers
tended at this time to be overrepresented in the ratings.
The most popular program of the mid-sixties was CBS's
"The Beverly Hillbillies," country folk who come to sophisticated Southern California and outslick the city dudes.
When Granny Clampett decided to fish in the swimming
pool of her fancy estate, she caught a toy plastic fish.
"There's Beverly Hills fer you! All flashy an' show on the
outside, but nothin' inside where it counts." During the
1960s, CBS presented so many variations on down-home
themes that it became known as the Hillbilly Network.

By the 1970s, the number of viewing hours had increased—and so had viewer dissatisfaction. The passage of
time and daily contact with the set had cooled the television audience's ardor. The first, uncritical stage of the affair was over; as Robert Bower concluded, the audience's
relationship with the set had become one of "somewhat
milder affection." People no longer were letting the

images unroll before them passively; there was, by the testimony of the ratings books, more channel switching and more conscious decisions to watch *specific* programs rather than television *qua* television. In certain respects, familiarity has bred a kind of contempt.

Television is still, in many respects, a great People Machine, whether it uses the older hard sell or the newer "real people" approach. But it can't sell *every*thing anymore. Television is no longer a novelty, a toy, or a technological wonder. It is now just one more of the "goods and services" of society. Or, as the critic Pauline Kael put it, television is just one of the appliances around the house.

Television has, in fact, half consciously instructed its audience in this respect. From its earliest days, television has frequently tried to take its viewers behind the scenes, demystifying its forms. In the 1950s, Dave Garroway walked onto a set with the lighting and cameras deliberately made visible in the background; Edward R. Murrow swiveled in his studio chair, placed by design in front of a bank of control room monitors. In the 1970s, the camera on the "CBS Evening News with Walter Cronkite" opens on the "actual" working space for the program; the CBS local news on the five stations it owns has been redesignated "Newsroom." The teletypes, assignment boards, coffee cups, and other paraphernalia of a real news operation are highly visible. There are no more plastic toy fishes, in a sense, but the viewer still recognizes the flash and show "on the outside." It is, in fact, still all part of *show* business (Does it make any difference if the news is delivered in a "working" newsroom?). The viewer also knows that it is all part of show *business,* the catching of crowds in order to sell them something.

The Awareness of Process

Advertisers have long understood that much of their mass advertising is devoted to products that are only marginally different ("Use our soap, it's rounder!"). The largest advertiser on television is Procter and Gamble, the detergent maker.[7] The rest of the top ten advertisers include the makers of drugs, automobiles, beer, toiletries, soft drinks, and telephones. But what advertisers know, their audience-students have also begun to learn as a result of the thousands of hours in the classroom of television: there isn't that much difference between the soaps—and six packs—touted on the screen. There is the strong suspicion that many of the products being pushed have little utility, marginal or otherwise (Does everyone really need a deodorant? Is racing car acceleration a good thing in passenger cars? Will waxed floors make me socially acceptable?). If the consumer movement signifies anything, it is that large numbers of "ordinary" people have begun to examine product claims skeptically.

Not long ago, Norman Mailer observed that "we've passed the point in civilization where we can ever look at anything as a work of art. There is always our knowledge of it and the making of it." When Mailer covered the Republican National Convention in 1972 and treated it like a television show, with Richard Nixon as director, he expressed in biting literary form what millions of viewers have been coming to realize. You no longer have to be an elite member like Norman Mailer—something Mailer airily overlooked—to have the knowledge of the artifice in a work. The years of watching television, as well as being exposed to other media sources, have produced an awareness of process on the part of the audience. This is why the making of commercials—or the making of presidents—is becoming a more chancy occupation.

———

Shortly after finishing the draft of this chapter, a letter arrived at the Washington television station where I appear as a critic-commentator on the evening news program. The letter sums up, so perfectly, the points I have been trying to make that I am reprinting it in full. Note that the writer is a very heavy viewer; he or she is familiar with both daytime and prime-time programming, with weeknight and weekend shows; he or she watches the news and public affairs programs regularly enough to know the names and assignments of several different people. Also note that the letter writer—who, I imagine, is older, high-school-educated, white, and "Middle American" (and therefore "typical" of the heavy-viewer television audience)—is a *critical* viewer, conscious of the performances and production values in both the news and the entertainment programs, despite some of the spelling and other errors:

Washington, D.C.
March 18, 1974

The Director
CBS-WTOP—Channel 9 TV
4001 Brandywine Street, N.W.
Washington, D.C.

Dear Sir:

Clean up your Station Channel 9; it's getting to dirty for family viewing.

Do you think that showing crazy 'streakers' running on campus is *news?* The kind that people want to see in their homes, and have their children see?

What do you think you obtained by showing 'One Night in Paradise?'

And that stupid showing of "Tell me where it hurts?" Of all the ridiculous arguments in favor of Women's Lib? The women in that picture were shown as having, at least, twenty years of married life—that brings us back to 1954— and do you think that *intelligent* women at that stage in life would be interested in discussing their sex ignorance of almost half a century earlier? Don't you think that intelligent women have more important things to think about *today?* I was in agreement with the husband who forbid his wife attending those 'talks'. It was about the biggest stupidity I have seen in a long time. I shut it off before it finished . . . I couldn't take it any longer!

As for that piece of dirt that comes under the heading of 'Maude' it should be wiped off the screen.

You also have too much police on your TV shows— Barnaby Jones—Gunsmoke—Cannon—Kojak—Hawaii 5— Mannix. Mannix is good; true there is some shooting, but Michael Conners is an excellent actor and he always fights clean.

Warner Wolf [the sports news editor] is excellent. He comes across so honestly, and in such a friendly way that he just makes one like him.

Why has our cheerful 'weatherman' been replaced by that nervous gentleman who never seems to be quite sure of what he is saying. We get the details thrown at us so quickly that we don't know if it is the rising tide or the setting sun, and what is the weather for the next day?

Maureen Bunyan [news reporter] made a good beginning, but why is she made to speak before the Court House or some other traffic-congested place where she is smothered out of hearing?

Why is Judy Siegler [news reporter] almost never shown? Her voice comes through a maze of traffic sounds, and then, at the end, there is barely a glimpse of her? She is a pretty girl and apparently a good reporter. Why don't you give your anchor men and women equal share?

As for Agornsky & Co. they should be told to go home . . . They are just five men who happen to be newspaper reporters, and who sit around giving their personal opinion on matters that in some instances are beyond them, and who never arrive at any intelligent conclusion. Any family could produce five members in their own circle to say similar things and no one would dream of paying them or giving them TV coverage.

Archie Bunker is a shouting match. His wife is too stupid for human consumption, his daughter Gloria is a shameless little snipet, and Michael seems to be the only acceptable one, although I give Archie the credit of being a good actor.

The World at War was a good showing. It was hard to take, at times, but those things really happened, and we have all lived through them, revolting as they were.

Good Times is a lot of good-natured nonsense, with the mother as the best actress of the group.

Mary Tyler Moore is consistently good.

The Bob Newheart show is excellent. Bob Newheart is an excellent actor.

As for Everywoman [daytime local women's program] . . . I have watched them for several weeks and I still fail to see what their objective is . . . What are they trying to get across?

As for "Six Rooms Riv-Vu" it was well acted and well written, but it was contaminating! It hadn't a redeeming quality. We felt as if muck from the street had been thrown into our living-room. . .

So, Mr. Director, clean up your showing on TV. We are sick of sex, and so much killing . . . Think of the vast quantity of material that could be made interesting for TV showing. . .

A disappointed Viewer

Chapter 3
Audiences: "Out There"

But will it play in Peoria?
—Question asked within the Nixon White House

The notion that the people in the Peorias of America respond in some manner different from urban or East Coast Americans has become an accepted part of current political wisdom. The Nixon years produced "the silent majority" and "Middle America." Theodore H. White speaks of "Out There" in his book on the 1972 presidential campaign. And Clifton Daniel, associate editor and Washington bureau chief of the *New York Times,* told a *Women's Wear Daily* reporter not so long ago:

You know, there is a tendency here in New York to make too much about "great issues." People out in the country are not quite so agitated about these things as we are. They don't intellectualize about them the way we do. They're busy planting their lawns . . . going to Disneyworld . . . getting the boat ready . . . living their everyday lives. Maybe it's a good thing they're not too concerned about what goes on. . . .

These descriptions, to my mind, have always had an unreal—as well as patronizing—sound; they seem like Madison Avenue's version of a "typical" American family in its television commercials—families held together by their shared use of liquid Prell shampoo. For a time, I half suspected that these descriptions were largely rhetorical; no serious, successful political strategy could be built on such an ill-defined base. But it seems that Richard Nixon himself saw the American electorate divided between the politicized "intellectuals" and the uncaring "average people." In one of the more revealing passages in the taped presidential conversations, Nixon (P) is discussing with John W. Dean III (D) the prospect of Senate hearings that would look more closely into the Watergate scandals:

P   Well, so be it. I noticed in the news summary Buchanan was viewing with alarm the grave crisis in the confidency of the Presidency, etc.

D   Well the best way—

P   How much?

D   Pardon?

P   How much of a crisis? It will be—I am thinking in terms of—the point is, everything is a crisis. (expletive deleted) it is a terrible lousy thing—it will remain a crisis among the upper intellectual types, the soft heads, our own, too—Republicans—and the Democrats and the rest. Average people won't think it is much of a crisis unless it affects them. (unintelligible)[1]

During the summer of 1973, the News Study Group at MIT and Wellesley College tried to find out, in a modest way, if the political picture of "Out There"—where most people supposedly ignore the public news that doesn't affect them directly—had any more basis in reality than the Prell people.[2] Specifically, we conducted panel studies, observing over an extended period and interviewing extensively a small number of "ordinary" Americans as the Watergate hearings were being held. We were particularly interested in their media consumption habits and their levels of awareness: how closely they followed the Watergate story (if indeed they did); why they reacted to specific events, testimony, or newsmakers. Finally, we wanted to learn what changes, if any, occurred in their political attitudes during the course of the summer. While we were

HEAD OF THE TIMES . . .CHANGIN

not literally in Peoria, Illinois, during the summer, we did
conduct interviews in working- and middle-class neighborhoods in East Longmeadow, Massachusetts; Frankton,
Indiana; Dayton, Ohio; Des Moines, Iowa; and Portland,
Oregon. We talked to over 50 people, men and women,
young and old, engineers and semiskilled assembly line
workers, Republicans, Democrats, and independents.

Ahead of the Times
The first general finding was that, contrary to any picture
of Middle Americans tending their lawns and dialing out
on the news, our panels paid close—even avid—attention
to the Watergate scandals throughout the summer. In
some cases, in fact, people "Out There" were able to follow the hearings more closely than the "upper intellectual
types." The blue-collar workers on the second shift at the
Delco-Remy plant in Anderson, Indiana, for example,
don't report to the assembly line until 4:30 P.M.; many
of them spent the day watching the televised Ervin committee hearings (as well as keeping up with the newspaper
accounts) and then discussed Watergate with each other
at work. On the West Coast, the time lag meant that Ore-
gonians could watch the morning sessions before going to
work; one small-business man in Portland delayed going
to his office until the morning hearings adjourned about
12:30 Washington time (9:30 on the West Coast). But
people all over in the panels watched regularly; in western
Massachusetts, of ten panelists, seven read about Watergate daily in the newspapers, and four watched the hearings regularly, especially the rebroadcasts at night on public television. Attention to the hearings was unexpectedly
high among people who had voted for Nixon in 1972. In

NDS AND HEARTS . . . HOW IT PLA

the engineering department of a large manufacturing plant in Dayton, there was only one McGovern voter in a group of 17 men holding managerial and foreman jobs; but a large majority of the group followed and approved of the hearings.

A second finding was that the hearings stirred strong emotions among people "Out There." In Iowa, inflation and farm prices were the overriding topics in the summer of 1973; but—again, contrary to many reports— concern about the bread-and-butter issues apparently *heightened* rather than blurred the impact of Watergate. Norman Sandler, one of our group who worked as a reporter in the state capital bureau of United Press International in Des Moines, found that people were following feed prices and phase four news in the national pages of Iowa newspapers, then turning to the Watergate stories in the adjoining columns. Furthermore, several people made a linkage between the "corruption of Watergate" and the "corruption of special interest policies" like the wheat sale.

A third finding was that panelists reacted, not surprisingly, to individual personalities rather than to broad constitutional issues. Many people formed their opinions about Watergate on the basis of the face on the screen. Senator Howard Baker of Tennessee was "impressive." Former Attorney General John Mitchell appeared as "more of a Godfather than The Godfather." Halderman-Ehrlichman lawyer John Wilson came across as "feisty." Senator Edward Gurney of Florida was "Nixon's boy." One fiftyish woman, a Nixon voter, was interviewed before, during, and after the testimony of John W. Dean III. About Dean, she concluded, "He can't be lying because he never makes a mistake. No one who was lying could

'ED IN PEORIA . . .BEYOND THE PU

be sure of every single detail . . . of every single date. . . ."
A middle-aged Oregonian, a milkman, concluded after
watching John Ehrlichman's testimony, "He's obviously
lying; look at his sweaty brow and the way he bites his
lip like a fish. . . ." There was relatively scant discussion
of the civil libertarian issues raised by the "plumbers'
unit," mail covers, wiretaps, or the office break-ins.

Other, more systematic surveyors of public attitudes
have observed this *personalization* process. At the crest
of the Watergate revelations, the opinion sampler Daniel
Yankelovich decided Nixon would be swamped and would
never recover. As Yankelovich explained it to Hugh Sidey
of *Time* magazine, Richard Nixon so permeated the media
"he became almost a member of everybody's family."[3]
And so while many people "don't always understand the
big issues," they do grasp a whole lot of little things about
the President that they can understand, like his tax returns
and his airplanes and his limousines.

Yet it is unwarranted to conclude that the "impersonal"
constitutional questions were somehow over the heads of
the people "Out There." The Watergate scandals, particularly the Watergate Special Prosecutor's efforts to obtain
the recorded presidential conversations—the celebrated
"battle of the tapes"—offered an unequaled opportunity
for news organizations to inform millions of their readers
and viewers about governmental processes in a vivid, even
melodramatic, way. An examination of the newspaper and
television accounts available to most Americans shows
that, in general, this "civics lesson" went untaught. The
news services may have sent out stories of analysis and interpretation, but relatively few of them showed up in the
tightly constricted national pages of regional newspapers.
Most daily coverage outside New York and Washington

C NEWS . . . "SOPHISTICATED" IGN

was—there is no other word for it—perfunctory. The early evening network news programs, limited as they may be, helped tie together and explain the testimony better than the regional newspapers. The pattern was one of the audience being ahead of its alleged leadership "elites" in the press and in Congress. For example, the "battle of the tapes" excited real attention among the "average people." Specific details about the tapes were widely known and discussed. However, the question more often than not was "Why did Alexander Butterfield tell about the tapes just then?" The wider questions of executive privilege and separation of powers were not really explored, though there was the gut feeling "Out There" that, as one Delco-Remy worker said, "The President can't disobey a court order because he's no better than anyone else."

Changing Minds and Hearts

Just how and why political attitudes change has been a matter of lively debate among communications researchers. One older body of research suggests that the mass media have relatively little effect on individual decision making compared to the personal influence of family and friends. Most of this work was done in the pretelevision era years of the 1950s, or earlier—for example, Paul Lazarsfeld's influential studies of voters in Erie County, Ohio, and Elmira, New York, were based on the 1940 and 1948 presidential elections.[4] Another, more popular position holds that skilled practitioners of the television arts can manipulate the attitudes—and subsequent voting behavior—of the audience. Supposedly, the less knowledgeable the viewer is about the subject at hand, the more susceptible he or she is to direct persuasion by the camera.

JRANCE

Our own work found some holes in both these positions.
People "Out There" tangibly changed their minds as a result of watching and reading about Watergate. One Massachusetts woman—Italian, Catholic, a high-school dropout
with four grown children—had voted for Nixon in 1972
because he was "more of a politician than McGovern,
more positive and a better decision maker. . . ." After
John Dean's testimony, the woman became convinced of
the President's involvement: "If he's implicated, let him
pay for it, let him go down with Benedict Arnold." The
President's nationally televised speech "explaining" his
role in Watergate on August 15, 1973, failed to move her.
She had hoped that "the truth might finally come out,"
but the President had been "evasive and passing the
buck. . . ." If he didn't resign, she said, he should be im-
peached. She had used the word, without swallowing, well
before the idea had become acceptable among the "more
attentive"—as the attitudinal surveyors put it—elite
publics.

Panel reaction to Nixon's August 15 speech was particularly instructive. In past television appearances, Nixon
had been quite effective in getting his message across—
the commander-in-chief effect discussed earlier. This rallying effect did not occur "Out There" during the summer
of 1973. MIT student Barbara Moore, observing a group
of engineers in Dayton, found that "everyone was anxious
to see Nixon's televised speech, and it was the topic of discussion for quite a while." Afterward, however, "absolutely no one in the office thought that the speech was convincing." Five said that they thought it did no harm; the
other twelve expressed varying degrees of anger or disap-
pointment over what they felt to be "Nixon's cop-out."

They wanted an explanation from him instead of what seemed to them to be evasions. By the end of the summer, there were at least eight avid anti-Nixon people in the group and only two admitted Nixon supporters. A foreman said, "Nixon's taken the confidence away even from those who voted for him. . . ."

How It Played in Peoria
In mid-October 1973, as it turned out, the MIT News Study Group actually did get a chance to see how events were playing in Peoria. On Saturday, October 20, Special Watergate Prosecutor Archibald Cox was forced out of his office by President Nixon; Attorney General Elliot Richardson and Assistant Attorney General William Ruckelshaus both resigned in protest. Two members of the News Study Group, Paul Schindler and Norman Sandler, visited Peoria the Sunday and Monday after this "Saturday Night Massacre." Using the Peoria telephone book, they telephoned and interviewed a dozen John Smiths and Mrs. John Smiths—as Middle American a name as they could find. They also interviewed in person a dozen other Peorians—business people, waitresses, gas station attendants, and other ordinary citizens.

The first finding was that the people in Peoria were well informed about the Watergate case, including the issues involved in the Special Prosecutor's request for the presidential tapes. Only two out of 23 people said they had not followed the events of the weekend. Almost half had learned quickly of the Cox firing and Richardson and Ruckelshaus resignations from radio and television (it was the weekend of the New York Mets–Oakland A's world series). Another finding was that only two of the 23

Peorians interviewed had anything vaguely positive to say about Richard Nixon. Most said their opinions had changed—for the worse. "I've lost faith in him," was a common remark. Several Peorians wondered about the President's emotional state. Without any prompting, the word "impeachment" came up naturally.

The Peoria sampling, obviously, was too small and impressionistic to be scientific. But the Gallup poll and a Quayle telephone survey that weekend produced similar results. There is also strong collateral evidence that the White House's own soundings began to pick up the same responses. The Archibald Cox firing had been set in motion by Cox's request to obtain certain of the tape-recorded presidential conversations. In the middle of the weekend, President Nixon's special legal counsel, Charles Alan Wright, was telling some people in Washington, "It worries me not at all that the White House is in non-compliance with the courts." The Columbus Day weekend was beginning, and many news executives watching the first announcements on Friday night were convinced that the President's men were trying to blunt the edge of events by the holiday-weekend timing. If the game plan figured on the public ignoring or stolidly accepting the story, it collapsed very fast. A "firestorm" of protest erupted. By the next Tuesday, Wright was assuring reporters that the President *would* supply the tapes.

Beyond the Public News
The intensity of the public reaction to the Saturday Night Massacre in the Peorias of the nation surprised the "elites" in Washington. "*We* feel this way," a man working for a U.S. Senate committee said at the time, "but

we didn't think *they* did. . . ." Like Richard Nixon, the
Senate aide had taken a somewhat condescending attitude
toward the "average people."

"Peoria," of course, is supposed to be a state of mind
rather than a physical place. "Average people" who have
no interest in national "crises" and national politics do
exist in large numbers. Even so, the picture is much more
complex than the overly simplistic map drawn by the
Nixon White House. Literally millions of Americans live,
by choice, outside the range of the public news. Paul
Cowan, a reporter for the *Village Voice*, spent a good deal
of time between 1967 and 1972 interviewing working-
class whites around the country. Most of the people
Cowan met were hardly citizens of the McLuhanesque
global village that television has supposedly created; they
were "more like strangers in a strange land . . . self-con-
tained groups of people who have not yet made the psychological transition from their ancestral homes in Italy,
Ireland, Israel, Latin America, Africa to the 1970s." Professor Penn Kimball of Columbia University, in an excellent study of the 1970 elections in Newark, New Jersey,
and other urban areas, found hundreds of thousands of
minority poor who rarely take part in political processes.
Kimball called them "The Disconnected."[5]

Citizens cut off from the public news live not just in
the ethnic neighborhoods of South Boston or East Los
Angeles or East Harlem. In 1971, when the Nixon Justice
Department brought Father Philip F. Berrigan and a
group of antiwar Radical Catholics to trial in Harrisburg,
Pennsylvania, there was a serious question about how fair
the trial could be. Surely, the argument went, it would be
difficult to find prospective jurors without strong opinions

about the Berrigans, about Catholic radicalism, or about
the Indochina War. As it turned out, there was no problem; several prospective jurors had no clear opinions
about any of these matters. Of 25 potential jurors out of
the first prospective panel of 42, only a few said they
made a daily habit of reading newspapers or listening to
the television news and the commentators. "I read only
the hunting and the fishing column and the funnies and
the people who died," explained a middle-aged steelwork-
er. He said he was so insulated from other events that he
became aware of the Indian-Pakistani War only when his
hunting companions mentioned it.

Since Harrisburg is rural, white, Protestant country, one
of the reasons that the Nixon Justice Department lawyers
sought the Berrigan indictment there in the first place,
some of this might not be so surprising. But the same
thing happened a few months later when prospective jurors were being impaneled for the Daniel Ellsberg–Anthony
Russo Pentagon Papers trial in Los Angeles; the city of
Los Angeles is perhaps the most media-saturated area in
the country, with seven television stations, dozens of
radio stations, and the "influential" *Los Angeles Times.*
Again, lawyers had no trouble finding jurors—this time,
well educated, professional, and young—who had never
heard about the Papers, the defendants, or the First
Amendment issue, despite the fact that the "historic"
case had gone all the way to the United States Supreme
Court and had dominated the news for a good part of the
summer of 1971. Similarly, the first trials resulting from
the Watergate scandals, certainly among the most extensively covered political events in decades, never lacked
for jurors without knowledge of some of the leading

characters. In 1973, at the impaneling of the jury for the trial of Dwight Chapin, the President's appointments secretary, only one in every three of the prospective jurors had ever heard of Chapin—and this in Washington, D.C.

Richard Nixon was partly correct in another respect. There are many people, "average" and "upper intellectual," who simply tune out the public news. They screen certain messages in a familiar process of selective perception; in effect, they are seeing or hearing only what matches personal beliefs. The more intensely these personal attitudes are held, the less likely they can be touched, let alone changed, by persuasive communication. The writer Gail Sheehy, in *New York* magazine, found people who didn't want to hear any "new" information when she went to Queens—"Archie Bunker Country"—to watch the Senate Watergate hearings at Terry's Bar in the summer of 1973:

Terry Bennett took a vote among a select group of the American people in his bar in Astoria, Queens. "Look, do you want me to put on that Watergate?" Ten men shouted, "Forget it." One didn't care. One said yes, being the kind of guy who would say anything to start a fight. The majority called for Popeye cartoons. But Terry couldn't find a channel that wasn't polluted with the "search for unvarnished truth." They had no choice.[6]

Television, Sheehy concluded, "was suppressing their freedom not to know."

"Sophisticated" Ignorance

There is another form of selective listening and seeing that may have been developing around the country in recent years. The Watergate hearings in 1973 received extensive coverage, and during that period, the public ratings of

Richard Nixon plummeted sharply, as we have seen. But
the standings of other politicians, Democrats as well as
Republicans, also dropped. After the first three months
of the Senate's Watergate hearings, involving 35 witnesses
and 7,500 pages of testimony, a Louis Harris poll showed
that a large majority of the American public agreed, at
that point in time, with the proposition that "dirty campaign tactics exist among Democrats and Republicans and
the Nixon campaign people were no worse, except that
they got caught at it. . . ." Seven out of ten Americans
adopted this remarkably wrong-headed conclusion even
though a mountain of information had been publicly ac-
cumulated about Republican "dirty tricks" and not one
molehill of information had been gathered about illegal
Democratic campaign tactics.

The belief that "everybody does it" reflects an attitude
about politics that, apparently, cannot be eroded by "information," no matter how good or how readily available
it is. Few journalists or social scientists would quarrel
with another proposition, set forth in the *New Yorker*
magazine during the Watergate hearings, that "probably
never before have the people of this country been as well
informed as they are now." But it is not true that "everybody does it." To say so is to replace one form of ignorance with another, more "sophisticated," ignorance. Both
attitudes are equally naive and without basis in "information."

Nevertheless, the skeptics' role is one that many people
increasingly cultivate. It is learned quite early in life. Professor Scott Ward, a marketing specialist at the Harvard
Business School, has reported that there is an important
"break point" in the attitudes of children around age
seven and eight.[7] By the second grade, a great many

children have begun to develop a certain skepticism about what they see on television. For example, when asked if commercials on television "always tell the truth," most children say "no" or "sometimes." As these children get older, Ward found, they tend to tune out or decrease their attention when commercials come on. A kind of immunity to information is built up.

A more carefully drawn map of "Out There" would show several groupings rather than some ill-defined collective "average." At the far end would be the disconnected; next, the disinterested and the determined, or, more accurately, the predetermined. In the middle would be the attentive audiences, some listening but immunized, others still open minded. At the other end would be the politically active and the elites, including the most attentive consumers of the news. At the one extreme, people would be less likely to vote and to be consumers of the news; private news would interest them but not the public news. Moving toward the other extreme, media consumption would increase, as well as political interest. In terms of numbers, the continuum would be a bell curve.

It is this attentiveness in the center that the "elites" failed to understand during the Watergate scandals. In October 1974, on the first anniversary of the Saturday Night Massacre, William Ruckelshaus recalled that the public's reaction to the Cox firing was "so much stronger" than he had anticipated that it left him with a "very strong feeling about the wisdom of the American people." That was essentially the intuitive conclusion that the News Study Group had reached one year before, on the basis of the same impressionistic evidence.

If the people in the Peorias of the country weren't the rubes they had been made out to be by the Nixon White House, how then is it possible to account for the election of Richard Nixon in 1968 and his overwhelming reelection in 1972? Certainly, it could be said that he played well in Peoria for a long time.

Perhaps not. Voting figures show that proportionately fewer voters have gone to the polls in presidential elections since 1960. In the 1972 Nixon-McGovern race, for example, 4 million *more* citizens voted in the governors' and senators' contests than for the presidential candidates. In all, 75 million people voted for Nixon or McGovern in 1972; 85 million had been expected to vote, out of the total of the estimated 140–150 million eligible citizens over eighteen years of age. Since some 75 million Americans *didn't* vote, it is possible to conclude, as the sociologist Amitai Etzioni did, that McGovern finished third, not second—and that Nixon came in second, not first.[8] In fact, according to Walter Dean Burnham of MIT, 1972 was the lowest turnout in American electoral history since 1948. The year 1972 might have made even more dubious history if there had not been permanent and large increases in the South's turnout in recent years as a result of the enactment of the Civil Rights Act of 1965. Excluding the eleven ex-Confederate states, the 1972 turnout in the rest of the country fell below 58 percent— about equal to the all-time lows of 1920 and 1924.

Perhaps the decline in presidential voting in 1972 was a sign of the developing immunity to public news in the public media. Or perhaps, given the major party choices, it was a measure of collective political wisdom. In our own work, we found nothing to support the idea that the citizens in the Peorias of the country are either passive or malleable. They read, they listen, they draw conclusions, although perhaps as much from feelings as from facts. As one Oregonian said to an interviewer, "We care."

It would be enormously helpful to the media consumer, of course, if the "elites" who produce the public news showed a similar sense of care. The following two chapters examine some of the implicit assumptions and institutional practices of the producers of the news.

Chapter 4
News Forms: The Network News

The three network early evening news programs—the "CBS Evening News with Walter Cronkite," the "NBC Nightly News" (John Chancellor), and the "ABC Evening News" (Harry Reasoner and Howard K. Smith)—have been around in their present form since 1963. In many respects, there is little to choose among them. They have grown to look like each other, the way old married couples and their dogs often come to resemble one another. In New York City, Cronkite, Chancellor, and Smith-Reasoner all go on the air at 7:00 P.M. and run for approximately 23 minutes and 30 seconds after the commercials and station bumpers (the identification slides) are subtracted. Usually, each program runs the same five or six film stories: Washington politics, war (Indochina, Cyprus, or Northern Ireland), news from the heartland, natural disasters (such as floods, storms, quakes, tornadoes), and unnatural disasters (the economy, food costs). All appear in just about the same sequence. The editing techniques are similar, even to the point of the wording of the in-cues and out-cues. "When you turn your dial back and forth between Channels 2, 4, and 7 during the film pieces you can't tell what network you're with," acknowledges Richard Wald, the president of NBC News. "Only the anchorman tells you where you are." A Cronkite or a Chancellor, says Wald, is the distinct orienting element—"the equivalent of the newspaper layout of *The New York Times* or the *New York Daily News;* when audiences see him they know where they are."

About 47 million people, over 40 million of them adults, watch Cronkite, Chancellor, or Smith-Reasoner on an average weeknight. Lyndon B. Johnson installed a triple-screen television rig in his White House offices so he could keep an eye on these "powerful" channels of information. Although Richard Nixon removed the sets from the Oval Office, a team of monitors working under Presidential Assistant Patrick Buchanan was assigned to video-tape-record and analyze *all* the newscasts on behalf of the President. When CBS or NBC or ABC ran a story or suggested a viewpoint that seemed to go counter to one or another of the Administration's positions, Buchanan and company would note it for the President's attention (a monitor once told me that after he had watched some Vietnam War coverage, he wanted to kick the set). Around the Nixon White House in its first four years, the phrase "Who Elected Sevareid?" was frequently used; who gave the CBS news commentator Eric Sevareid—or any other network correspondent—the right, the President's men asked, to speak against the President to millions of citizens every night from the towering platform of national television?

The concern of Lyndon Johnson and of President Nixon's men was probably genuine. It was also, given the nature of the news on television, probably quite unnecessary.

The Audience for National News

In recent years, significant numbers of viewers apparently have decided *not* to watch the national news. Around the network news operations, there is a certain uneasiness, perhaps no bigger than a Nielsen rating point, about the

HE AUDIENCE FOR NATIONAL NE

future. It seems that some natural demarcation point has been reached in the life of the network news. In early 1973, for example, the annual du Pont-Columbia broadcast survey prominently reported that the audience for the three networks' evening news programs had dropped from 25.6 million households in February 1971 to 24.7 million households in February 1972.[1] In the same year, however, the number of television sets in the country had steadily increased by almost 2 million, to 62.1 million, and the use of sets had also climbed to record highs: on an average winter day, the average set was on almost seven hours. The equally bad news, tucked away in a footnote in the survey, was that viewers per household had been dropping when the network news was on, from 2.0 viewers in 1968 to 1.7 in 1972. That slippage, a seemingly small matter, meant that fewer bodies last year were "Out There" watching the network news—and the sponsors' messages—compared with four years before.

The Department of Research at ABC News challenged the du Pont-Columbia figures, arguing that the reported drop in news viewing was only for one rating period in 1972 and that over the entire year, Cronkite, Chancellor, and Smith-Reasoner had, cumulatively, *gained* 1 million households.[2] The ABC researchers also cited figures to show that the "audience growth trend to network news" continued in 1973. The network evening news ratings for the first five months of 1974, however, showed a *drop* of about 662,000 households, or over 1 million viewers nightly (see p. 62).

Some of the reasons for the dips and shifts in audience attention undoubtedly have little to do with the quality of the newscasts: in the first two years of the second

. . . DEMANDING COMMUNICATION

Households Watching Network News, 1971–1974

Numbers are notoriously slippery, but, for the record, the figures claimed for the three network news programs in four recent January ratings periods are shown here.

Households Watching	1971	1972	1973	1974
ABC	5,290,000	6,710,000	7,390,000	7,330,000
CBS	10,880,000	9,690,000	10,170,000	9,877,000
NBC	9,200,000	8,570,000	9,660,000	9,540,000
Total	25,370,000	24,970,000	27,220,000	26,747,000

Source: ABC News.

Nixon Administration, there was an almost unbroken run of crises, as insistent as an Excedrin headache, and it may be that people can take only so much depressing news ("Weariness with Watergate," proclaimed the subheadline on the *New York Times* account of the 1974 drop). Furthermore, the Federal Communications Commission's maladroit access rule (limiting the number of programs a network can supply) continued to separate the early-evening network newscasts from the temporary relief, for some people, of the prime-time entertainment shows. This had the effect of undermining any strong lead-out benefits to the news programs. And, finally, the steady batterings of the Nixon Administration had succeeded in chipping away some of the credibility—and, apparently, audience—of the evening news.

Demanding Communications
But, just as clearly, the form of the network news itself has contributed to viewer restlessness. The 23-minute

... 1950s FRINGE NEWS ... 1960s H

format is too short and stylized; not even the featured stars defend it with any enthusiasm. "We can't tell the whole story," John Chancellor has said. "A television news program is a special sort of front page."

It is important to understand just how special the news on television is. A newscaster speaking at a normal broadcast quality pace can deliver no more than 120 words a minute; the average, high-school-educated person can read about 250 words a minute. One night a few years ago, Richard Salant, the president of CBS News, in a well-publicized experiment whose discouraging outcome he could predict, had the entire script for the "CBS Evening News with Walter Cronkite" set in newspaper type. Salant found that the entire broadcast filled less than two columns of the first page of the *New York Times*. Anyone who has ever prepared or delivered a television broadcast, as I have over a period of five years, knows how difficult it is to make facts known or events understandable. Analysis is downright discouraging; one night in mid-1972 in Washington right after I delivered a carefully crafted (or so I thought), strongly worded commentary attacking then-Vice-President Spiro Agnew for his views on the press, a woman viewer telephoned the station to thank me for supporting the Vice-President. Any viewer who has tried to listen to television news knows how hard it is to follow the thread of all but the simplest narratives. For example, when the United States Supreme Court ruled in July 1974 that President Nixon had to turn over certain tapes of his recorded presidential conversations to the Watergate Special Prosecutor, the networks interrupted their regular programming to broadcast the news. Four different people who heard the same

DLINE SERVICES . . . THE NEXT DE

news bulletin all got the headline correct—the vote was 8 to 0—but they offered four different versions of what the court had ruled about executive privilege. Yet these viewers were largely blameless. Television's detractors argue that it is the "boob tube," that it requires a minimum of intelligence to use ("You don't even have to know how to read"). Actually, television is a very demanding mode of communication. Television information is ephemeral; there is no way for the viewer to go back over material, in the way a newspaper reader or book reader can glance back over the page. The television news program is, in the analogy of Richard Salant, table d'hôte rather than à la carte: the consumer has to sit through all the news to get what he or she wants; the viewer cannot go right to the desired item and skip over the rest of the menu.

Finally, the network news—local news may be another matter (see Chapter 5)—is *by definition* information of only indirect interest to the "average" viewer, as he or she perceives it. Edward Jay Epstein, in his study of the NBC news organization, picked an apt title: *News From Nowhere*. The viewer's neighborhood, job, family, friends, and personal concerns are seldom, if ever, directly involved in the 23 minutes of *global* news.

We also sense that while some national news, such as federal action (or inaction) affecting the rate of inflation, directly concerns many viewers, even then they may not follow Washington developments closely. This is not a matter of alienation, or apathy, or feelings of inefficacy; it is simply a matter of interest. When I made this point to a group of engineers in Cambridge, Massachusetts, not long ago, a young woman in the group wrote me her thoughtful response. It is worth quoting:

VELOPMENTS IN TV NEWS . . . FRO

One point you brought out and is a fairly common point is the seeming apathy of the public in general toward the day to day affairs of government. Having grown up in a small town in Michigan, let me suggest one possible reason for this on the part of some of the citizens and to do so let me make an analogy. Many people buy automobiles *only* as a means of transportation and have no interest in how it works, if the color is red or blue, etc. and the only time these people become at all involved in how the garage services the car is when it does not fulfill this basic transportation need.

The point is that some people may well view our government as a function to take care of certain needs and really do not want to be involved with the day to day carrying out of this function any more than the servicing of his car. And although that is often viewed with alarm by those who for various reasons have an interest in the day to day workings of the government, the other fellow may well feel he pays good taxes so that certain functions can be taken care of and he has no personal hobby-like intrigue with the government process and really wants to spend some of his free time and $ doing things which appeal to *him personally* and he probably can't understand why anyone would want to get all wrapped up in the governmental process when there is fishing, T.V., little league, etc.

Much of this would seem to be obvious. But when Andrew Stern, a former television news producer, joined the faculty of the University of California graduate school of journalism at Berkeley a few years ago, he looked in vain through the "communications literature" for specific studies of the effectiveness of the television news. While working for the networks and producing documentaries for public television, Stern recalls, "I had always wondered what people were getting out of our efforts."[3] In April 1971, Stern put together an experiment testing what people in the San Francisco area remembered from the evening news on television. His

ARROWCASTING TO BROADCASTI

method was simple. Every evening, Stern and his Berkeley students monitored all three network newscasts in the San Francisco area. On blackboards they listed each story, its length, and whether or not it was on film. In this way the interviewers had a complete rundown of each program. They then divided the responses of viewers when telephoned into two categories—aided recall and unaided recall. Those viewers who claimed to have watched a particular broadcast were first asked what stories, if any, they remembered. After this, they were read the list of stories and were asked which they remembered. If they remembered one, then they were asked for some detail to identify it. The interviewer then rated each viewer's level of recall. Interviewers were instructed to tell the respondents that there was no hurry in answering, that there were no "right" or "wrong" answers, and to wait patiently for an answer.

On the first question, "What do you recall from tonight's broadcast?" 51 percent said they didn't recall any stories. Those who did remember usually recalled more than one story. On the average, people remembered one story per newscast, or 6.2 percent of the program, given 19 stories per newscast. On the question of aided recall—that is, after the interviewer read off some headlines—the response was better. On the average, people recalled 4 stories without any details plus 4 additional stories with some details or facts. The overall recall for this part of the sample was 9 out of 19 stories.

In order to test whether or not people were correctly reporting their recall, Stern decided during the second week to add a nonexistent "story" about a police scandal in Phoenix, Arizona. Eleven people claimed recalling this story, out of 135 interviewed.

NG . . . GOOD NIGHT, WALTER, DA

April 1971 was a period of intense political activity: there were troubles in East Pakistan, the Nixon Administration had begun its diplomatic contact with Mainland China, Vietnam War protesters were rallying in Washington. Against this background, what was the recall rate for the editorial commentary of the feared Eric Sevareid by his "electors"? According to Stern, people almost never remembered the subject of a Sevareid, Smith, or Reasoner commentary (at the time of the study David Brinkley had not yet started his commentary on NBC). Out of 15 commentaries given during this period, only 6 viewers remembered the subject matter without help. They did slightly better with help. Feature stories also tended to have a lower recall rate, despite the length of time or film given to them. For instance, CBS's Charles Kuralt took almost five minutes for a story on hobo trailers and their owners' life-styles. The story had less than a 50 percent recall rate. All the lead stories did much better, including a 55-second story on Soviet cosmonauts linking up in orbit, with 80 percent recall; Vietnam veteran protesters scattered on Capitol Hill (on film), 135 seconds, 98 percent recall; a 140-second film story on plans for a mass demonstration against Attorney General John Mitchell, 60 percent. Even a 90-second film story on Haitian dictator François Duvalier's funeral scored high (70 percent). On ABC News that night, the same stories scored high, while its only feature and second-longest film story of the night (3 minutes, 10 seconds)—a report on the opening of a play about the trial of the Catonsville Nine, an antiwar group—had only a 27 percent recall rate. Stern says it is difficult to come to any firm conclusions about so-called soft news since the NBC soft news feature, a 2-minute, 15-second fluff piece about springtime in Washington, had about an 85 percent recall rate:

JOHN, HOWARD, HARRY

Stern also found that recall was vastly improved when the networks spent time and money on "the big story." For example, during Stern's monitoring period, both NBC and CBS News carried seven- to eight-minute reports on the American Ping-Pong team's visit to China. The reports were "satellite feeds"—film transmitted via Pacific Ocean communication satellite to the United States. The recall rate for that story was 90 percent on NBC and almost 70 percent on CBS. Another finding was that viewers had a hard time watching uninterruptedly the early evening network news—that great crowd collector that White House occupants worry so much about. Of those responding in Stern's sample, one-third said that they watched the whole news program; one-third watched the whole program but were distracted from time to time by various goings-on in the household; and one-third watched only part of the program because of serious distractions that drew them away from the set for a time. In the "seriously disrupted" category, viewers reported that they watched on the average of 16 minutes. Dinner was the major disrupting factor, accounting for one-third of the disruptions; other disruptions included the telephone, children, visitors, reading a book or newspaper while watching, and, last but not least, falling asleep. Unfortunately, we were not able to find out which stories put them into such a state. Some people said they had intended to fall asleep while watching television.

1950s Fringe News

Common sense suggests that there is nothing really startling in these findings. If the network evening newscasts were longer, then there might be more news from "somewhere." More time and money would mean more opportunity to give the "big stories" sufficient scope. If the networks scheduled the news at a time other than the dinner hour—when so much is going on in the typical household—then viewers would be somewhat better able to give the demanding, ephemeral images the attention they require.

But the problem goes beyond the time constraints of the medium, real as they are. The second important characteristic about television news is that it is only a part of the business of broadcasting. Most discussions about the "impact" of television seem to assume that the medium somehow exists for the dissemination of news and information. In fact, television, like radio before it, was conceived, born, and developed as a selling medium. It has never denied that character. The National Broadcasting Company, the first radio network, was started in 1926 by the Radio Corporation of America in part to encourage the sale of RCA radios. Soon broadcasters found that they had something much more valuable to market—the selling of audiences to advertisers. The bigger the audience, the more the advertiser could be charged. On strictly economic grounds, the requirements of successful broadcasting were quite straightforward: popular entertainment shows could earn higher revenues than less popular entertainment, news, or public affairs programming. The Federal Communications Act required some programming in the public interest, and news filled that requirement; it was an afterthought, to be done inexpensively, if possible, in fringe time. So it was with radio, and so it was with television—until quite recently.

Twenty-five years ago the biggest names in television

news were NBC's John Cameron Swayze (the "Camel News Caravan") and CBS's Douglas Edwards. The programs were 15 minutes long. They combined radio techniques—one man speaking into a microphone—with film made for theater newsreels. Swayze had a rapid-fire delivery ("Now let's go hopscotching the world for headlines!") suited to the movie newsreel. Both men read wire copy—or quick-laundered wire copy—with no pretense of ever having seen what they were talking about. The film was shot in the traditional Pathé or Hearst Movietone style: people getting on or off planes, three-alarm fires, news conferences. In 1963, the networks increased the evening news to 30 minutes (and later to Saturday and Sunday newscasts). The newsreel reader was demoted; a "real newsman"—Walter Cronkite had worked for UP during the war, David Brinkley was once a newspaper reporter—held together, or anchored, the film pieces and the spoken items.

1960s Headline Services

The old melodramatic newsreel style gave way; at CBS News, the playing of music "behind" the program credits was forbidden. Television news put on a serious, sober, straight mien: *New York Times*-style news. To signify the gravity of the new 30-minute network newscast, Cronkite conducted an exclusive interview with President John F. Kennedy on the first program. There was no doubt what new model television had taken for itself. To paper over (almost literally) the news on television, Cronkite called himself the "managing editor" of the CBS evening news; at CBS, too, Cronkite's studio set was built to look like the rim of a newspaper copy desk (though no managing

editor of a paper with over 20,000 circulation ever sat at
the copy rim). The networks went outside their organizations to hire news executives from the *New York Herald
Tribune*, *Colliers*, *Newsweek*, and United Press, among other
print backgrounds. By their own admission, they were
engaged in a "headlines service." If viewers wanted the
whole story, they were advised to go to their newspapers
the next morning.

Washington coverage during this print era of television
received the preponderant attention of the network news
organizations. CBS and NBC, for example, assigned up-
ward of twenty full-time correspondents to Washington—
as many as news organizations like the *New York Times*
or *Time* magazine. But while the figure was fully one-
third of a network's worldwide editorial staff, it represented no more than 4 or 5 percent of the *Times*'s or
Time's editorial staff. And even in Washington, the network newspeople functioned not as political correspondents but as White House or congressional reporters. Sur-
veying the political news coverage of the 1960s, Frederick
Sontag and John S. Saloma III in a Twentieth Century
Fund study concluded:

Television and radio news treat politics as a seasonal
phenomenon, mobilizing their resources for blitz coverage of the national conventions and elections. This cycli-
cal, sporadic attention to politics is accentuated by the
failure of the networks to add full-time political reporters
and analysts to their broadcasting and news-bureau staffs
who can provide continuous in-depth coverage of politics.
Only ABC of the three commercial television networks
had a political editor, William H. Lawrence, and even his
title was changed to National Affairs Editor. Instead, the
networks have supplemented their staff elections and conventions units with political consultants who periodically

offer comments during the extended coverage of the conventions or election returns but who are rarely called upon for regular network news programs. The almost inevitable consequence of leaving political coverage and commentary to the network anchor men is a superficial treatment of political news.[4]

The half-hour print era of TV news began with NBC's team of Chet Huntley and David Brinkley on top of the ratings. By the end of the 1960s, however, hundreds of thousands of viewers were dialing out on Huntley-Brinkley and switching to Cronkite. Within the terms of the competition, Cronkite was perceived by viewers to be the better—and more trusted—serious newsman. Paul Klein has since argued that the audience turned to Cronkite because he calmed their fears at a time when blacks, longhairs, hippies, yippies, and liberationists of all sorts shouted from the screen. Cronkite's success also suggested to some that the viewer wanted something other than straight "newspaper news" from television. Av Westin, who became executive producer of the "ABC Evening News" in 1969, decided this was a need for *reassurance*. The "average" home viewer, Westin concluded from his own experience, wants to know right away, in headline form, mainly two things: first, is my home safe and, second, is the world safe for the next 24 hours? The model was still print, though more *Daily News* style than *Times* style. And it seemed to work. In early 1973, according to ABC, the "ABC Evening News" program was getting something like a 21 percent share of the audience, versus 27 percent for CBS and 25 percent for NBC (the remaining 27 percent of sets in use were dialed to entertainment or movies on independent channels). Three years before, the ABC share was just 14 percent.

Star-struck television people like to argue that the ABC surge demonstrates the continued viability of the network news and its face on the screen, or in this case two faces. A more likely, though less discussed, reason was that "ABC Evening News" increased its ratings by increasing its clearances, that is, the number of affiliated stations that carry the newsfeed from New York. (The independently owned affiliates and the network, as Erik Barnouw explained in *The Golden Web*, the second volume of his definitive history of broadcasting, are linked only by contracts—and the telephone lines of AT&T. The network is the entrepreneur who creates the programming and sells the time to the advertisers; the affiliate elects, usually, to take the AT&T "feed" and shares in the advertising revenues.) In 1970, 124 stations cleared the "ABC Evening News"; in 1973, the figure was 187. "They are on almost as many 'newsstands' as we are," acknowledged John Chancellor. "And their circulation has accordingly risen."[5] Smith and Reasoner didn't get ABC on those newsstands by dint of personality, ability, or great news sense. They were helped considerably by ABC's network time salesmen who not only made the usual offers of "compensation"—in the form of the customary rebates from network advertising revenues—to stations taking the network offerings, but also emphasized, mainly to southern and southwestern stations, ABC's status as the Nixon Administration's least unfavorite network.

ABC's newspeople took no part in this sales pitch; the "ABC Evening News" is a professionally produced program with coverage, in Washington and elsewhere, little different from its rivals. And that, of course, is the point.

The only real movement in the network news in the last few years has been in ABC's clearances; now that this surge appears to be spent, ABC can't reasonably expect to pick up many more newsstands because there aren't that many eligible unaffiliated stations left. At the same time, the Cronkite program ratings have leveled off, and NBC's ratings remain largely static.

The on-air appearance of the three news programs reflects this feeling of stasis. The networks feverishly pursue marginal differences. The promotion material for the "ABC Evening News" says it has improved its background slides and other graphics "to heighten the impact of the news while helping the viewer to better identify and absorb complex events." The program ends with "commentary" by Howard K. Smith or Harry Reasoner. This is supposed to be significantly different from Eric Sevareid's "analysis" on CBS and David Brinkley's "Journal" on NBC, both of which are free to appear anywhere on the show, wherever they logically relate to the news. CBS uses a "clicker" technique at the beginning of the program to give the story lineup in 15 seconds; at the "ABC Evening News," a CBS executive points out triumphantly, the lineup takes a full minute! At the "NBC Nightly News," there has been considerably more tinkering with the studio sets, the executive producers, and the on-camera people in an attempt to regain the old preeminence. John Chancellor believes further change has to come "in the substance of the news." But when Chancellor becomes specific, he talks about techniques: "We have to find ways to discuss the news, not preach it . . . we need better writing, better selection of the stories, better organization, and more reporters' freedom. . . ."

It is hard to quarrel with these aims or with the other changes at the other networks. But they are, essentially, changes in the *furnishings* of the news. And the furnishings remain very much alike. The difference between *analysis*, *commentary*, and a *journal* are, at best, marginal. In television news, as in any other art form, incessant fussing with manner, rather than matter, is usually clear evidence of sterility; it marks the exhaustion of a style. The heads of the network news organizations are intelligent men; they don't need outside critics or stagnant ratings to remind them of what they can see with their own eyes: the news on television offers people information of (perceived) remote events, in an inappropriate form, at a time and in a style that makes it hard to absorb. A number of factors, however, are beginning to exert a tremendous pull on network television, and they may jolt the news organizations out of their old ways sooner than anyone expects.

The Next Developments in TV News

One factor is technology. "The real future of television lies in new technology," Richard Wald says. "The whole trend is to make equipment smaller, simpler, faster and more flexible." In the 1960s, a variety of new hardware—most importantly, videotape but also satellite relays, high-capacity undersea cables, and lighter cameras—began to change the old newsreel look of television. Wald believes that transformation will be completed—"in ways that I can't predict exactly"—by such new equipment as extremely lightweight cameras, one-inch videotape, and portable tape machines. Among the most promising developments is a versatile new color television camera called Minicam at CBS and PCP-90 at NBC. The Minicam or PCP-90 operates in two modes—first, as a portable tape recorder shooting one-inch videotape that can be motor-cycled back to the studio and immediately put on the air, and second, as a camera beaming pictures of an un-folding event right onto home screens via microwaved signals, a so-called "live remote." On April 24, 1973, CBS News had its Minicam pointed in mode one at Presi-dent Nixon when he broke his silence on Watergate at a 4:15 P.M. White House briefing; at 5:30 P.M., the state-ment appeared on WTOP-TV, CBS's Washington affiliate, with perfect broadcast quality. During the Watergate trials, the cameras were used for live remotes from the federal courthouse. Together with miniaturized tape and editing equipment, the camera can be fitted into vehicles no larger than Volkswagen microbuses, to serve as roving television stations. In a few years, the Telephone Com-pany will be able to install permanent sockets in the base of street telephone poles, permitting live television broad-casting simply by plugging in on the line; in a city the size of New York, 30 to 40 such street plugs might be installed. These street plugs could drastically alter the kind and the amount of material that could get on the air, taking the news farther from the studio and "manag-ing editor." The evening news, at a guess, could come to resemble the kind of television event the medium does best, the multiple switching and pickups of the political convention coverage.

The second pull on the network news is the changing economics of broadcasting. More and more, the news can be profitable. In a "bottom line" business like broadcast-ing, where the parent companies have set profit goals for *all* their divisions, and where the company stock is publicly traded, the importance of this development cannot be overstated.

There are three kinds of time on television: the affiliates' time, the network entertainment time, and the news time. Swayze and Edwards came on in the early edge of prime time (that period between 7:30 and 11:00 P.M. EST when most people are able to watch). Gradually, news was pushed out of the prime-time period and programmed by the networks so that they could "strip in" entertainment programs to attract larger audiences and therefore larger advertising revenues. When the networks scheduled their 15-minute news broadcasts—and later the 30-minute broadcasts—in the affiliates' time slots, each network gained 2 minutes and 30 seconds of advertising time per 15-minute block. These extra 5 minutes of commercials, each day, at rates of more than $30,000 per minute (depending on the ratings), can bring in $30 million to $40 million a year in added revenues to each network. The affiliates receive a portion of this revenue, about 30 percent, as compensation for surrendering their own time. But they aren't likely to give up any more time; when they do their own local news programming, they can keep 100 percent of the advertising revenues. The affiliates also know that if a news organization doubles the number of hours of news programming, its utilization of facilities becomes more efficient, and consequently the average cost of programming drops by as much as 40 percent. This explains, in part, why local news programs have expanded from 15 to 30 to 60 to 90 minutes, and to 120 minutes in Los Angeles and New York.

It also explains why there are still 23 minutes of "news from nowhere." The affiliates' unwillingness to surrender any more of their time hems in the network news on one side of the broadcast day. But the situation involving the parent network on the other side has changed, and news may make sense in network entertainment time. The cost of producing prime-time entertainment shows has been rising to $125,000 and more for a half-hour production, and the cost may go even higher if a change is engineered in the Federal Communications Commission rules regulating the number of reruns allowed. News can be produced for considerably less per half hour.

The third force upsetting conventional notions of the news is the demography of broadcasting; the audience of television is changing. Television advertisers used to be devoted solely to raw numbers. Now they increasingly want—and can get—good demographic distribution: relatively younger, better-educated, upper-income adults. The news audience used to be dominated by older people and blue-collar workers; there are some signs that it is shifting to the new "premium viewer" most desired by advertisers. Unfortunately, the networks have been slow to capitalize on the changing demographic distribution. Many potential premium viewers may not even be home when the network news is on the air—in Chicago, for example, the Cronkite program comes on at 5:00 P.M. The premium audience is at home after dinner and often watches the 11:00 P.M. news and the late-night Carson-style talk shows. Also, NBC has discovered that there is money to be mined in the hours *after* 1:00 A.M. NBC's "Midnight Special," at 1:00 to 2:30 A.M. on Friday nights, or rather Saturday mornings, has had good ratings as well as good demographic distribution (62 percent of the audience is in the eighteen- to forty-nine-year-old bracket, as compared to the prime-time average of 44 percent).

The pursuit of this younger, more intelligent audience could upset the current illogic of nighttime television programming. "Whoever said that the news doesn't belong in prime time is wrong," the head of one independent station group says. "The best programming that the networks do is their news." He thinks the networks should move news into prime time—like most every other affiliate, this man isn't yielding any of *his* station's time—and increase it to 45 minutes or 60 minutes. "They'll find a profitable audience there. . . ." In theory, network news executives agree. The ideal time for the news, Wald says, is later in the evening, about 10:30 to 11:30 P.M., "when people are closing out the day"—and when the dinner-hour distractions are over and the premium viewers are able to watch. Richard Salant thought, for a time during the 1969–1970 season, that CBS News could get the 7:00 to 8:00 P.M. time period. But in 1971, the FCC's access rule, designed to encourage "localism" and program "diversity," took the 7:30 to 8:00 P.M. time period from the networks, forbade network offerings in the period, and gave the time to the affiliates. The FCC had hoped that viewers would gain a wide variety of programming once the seven hundred plus stations in the country were free to strip in their own productions. Instead, almost every station purchased syndicated entertainment shows and the schlock game shows made by independent producers—the bottom of the barrel in television. More important, the stations had gained up to five minutes of commercial time for their own local advertising sales—and few seem willing to surrender those minutes again.

There is a fourth pull on the networks. The most profit-minded executive in broadcasting is still not a pure economic being. He is moved, like most men and women, by other "nonrational" drives: the desire for prestige, the approval of peers, "satisfaction" in work, the need for status ("a drive that may go deeper than politics or religion," the critic Pauline Kael has observed). In the past, when television had been imitative of newspapers, it had copied mainly their worst habits. The brilliant sappers' work done by the *Washington Post*'s Carl Bernstein and Robert Woodward to break the Watergate dam wide open underlined just how little investigative reporting the network news organizations have done in the past several years. "It was a little embarrassing, crediting the newspapers night after night on our broadcasts," a network executive said about the period of Watergate revelations. While the powerful megaphones of the evening news helped spread the word about Watergate, the network news organizations have been Easy Riders on the backs of other Washington reporters. More original reporting can be expected, for pride's sake if nothing else.

From Narrowcasting to Broadcasting

If technology, economics, demography, and the unpredictable force of personal motives push the networks toward longer, late-hour news programs, this prime-time news will have to be a different kind of news, with a different makeup. It is not merely a matter of offering more film pieces, although that certainly will be one bonus. Nor is it only a matter of expanding the present two- or three-minute items to four or six minutes, although longer items, when circumstances demand, will be needed. To program effectively—that is, *competitively*—in prime time, the network news organizations will also have to move into areas they have heretofore largely ignored because of their constricted view of television news as a newspaper headline service. Time and again, "missing" audiences keep appearing when fresh programming is offered. The network television day used to begin in mid-morning and end before midnight until a minor genius at NBC named Sylvester "Pat" Weaver thought up the "Today" and "Tonight" shows. The Senate Watergate hearings in 1973 and the House Judiciary Committee's impeachment debates in the summer of 1974 both attracted fresh viewers to sets.

In a way, television news has been narrowcasting rather than broadcasting. "Where is it written that the network news all has to be hard news?" a television executive told me. If the best thing television does is the news, then the best news programs done are "actualities"—real events, like political debates and congressional hearings. But right now, in 23 minutes, the networks don't even do sports "actualities" in a nation of sports freaks. "And what about commentary of a really diverse kind?" the executive adds. "Perhaps two or three people giving opinion? Sevareid and Brinkley don't really say that much. And what about reviews of Broadway, films, art, music, concerts . . . ?"

Finally, almost every critic returns to the problem of the overall static feeling of the network news—with the managing editor, or chief correspondent, firmly anchored in a studio rather than in reality. The value of the face

on the screen reading the headlines is overrated. Sooner
or later, the network news programs will have to break
away from their newspaper sets.

Of course, such radical change won't come quickly at
the networks. Television news is scarcely twenty-five
years old and is already as atherosclerotic as the newspaper business in many respects. One of television's key
articles of faith is that an entertainment show of any
kind (the fifth rerun of "I Love Lucy") will always out-
draw a news program, and advertising agencies are highly
conservative forces. They may give lip service to the
desirability of "upscale" demography, but in their hearts
they still worship raw numbers and the lowest possible
"cost per thousand" in buying an audience. And the
conventional wisdom still holds that the current star
system is essential. "If you abolish one man, someone
else will emerge," Wald says. "People like it. . . ." "You
need an anchorman to tell stories without film, and the
late-breaking news," Salant adds. "You can't have a
bunch of guys sitting on a set taking turns giving the
national news. . . ."

Given these considerations, the networks aren't likely
to plunge into a new kind of prime-time news programming without a great deal of temperature taking and toe
dipping. The real experimenting, as a matter of fact, has
been going on at local stations across the country. Critics
have fastened on to some of the surface idiocies of the
"Eyewitness News" format—the blazers, the music, the
sometimes clumsy attempts to liven things up—"Eyewit-
less News" the critic "Cyclops" has called it. But
Cyclops loses sight of the deeper efforts to create a genuine television news form in place of the old 1950s news-

reel or the 1960s newspaper of the air. Interestingly, Al
Primo, the "father" of "Eyewitness News," is one of the
few network news executives with absolutely no print
experience; all his professional life—he was born in 1935—
Primo has been around television studios.

Good Night, Walter, David, John, Howard, Harry
The trend has been to make news delivery less portentous.
More to the point, the "Eyewitness News" approach
helps shift the balance from headlines and the star on
camera to film, to the reporters in the field, and to the
story itself. One of the chief challenges of television
news has always been to make events understandable
through a medium—spoken words accompanying moving
pictures—that is superb for conveying emotions but practically opaque for the transmission of sustained thought.
Good film, good story selection, and good writing can
help, but other ways must be found to engage the audience. It doesn't take much research to realize that people
aren't watching television as if they were in a classroom
lecture with their notebooks open.

A number of critics have recognized that television
news needs a new makeup—one independent of newspaper models and, indeed, of anchormen. Paul Klein
thinks the entire star system of television news is over:
"Every long running show must come to an end; *Life
With Father* eventually closed on Broadway; and *Life
With Walter* will close, too. . . ."

Life with*out* Walter . . . and without John, and David,
and Harry, and Howard? It is really not unthinkable. The
fading of the broadcast news superstar, like suns whose
fires have burned low, and the change in the presentation

of the "front page" news would complete a natural evolution in the development of television journalism. Longer news, later in the evening, with more film and more "actualities," would, at the very least, give the viewer a chance to absorb the information offered—and perhaps even recall some of it. "Until the network news is longer," Fred Friendly once remarked in an interview, "the viewer will continue to be short changed. . . ." In fact, the national networks need look no farther than their own stations and affiliates in Los Angeles, in New York, and in Washington, where the length of the news programs has been increased to 60, 90, and 120 minutes—and the size of the news audience has also increased. In the local stations, then, it may be possible to see some of the shape of the future of television news. It is, as we shall see, a somewhat ambiguous prospect.

Chapter 5
News Forms: The Local News

Bill Greeley of *Variety* once called WNBC in New York "the world's richest television station."[1] Nothing about "NewsCenter 4," the two-hour news program in New York that NBC started in the spring of 1974, detracts from that reputation. The eighteen months of planning and testing with sophisticated audience research techniques, the sumptuous $300,000 set, the generous salary scales for on-air talent, the 200-person staff—the largest group anywhere putting out a news program, national or local—and the overall program budget of perhaps $12 million a year are all first class, even by NBC's big-spender standards.

The intention was to restore some measure of profitability and prestige to WNBC, where the early evening news ratings had dropped alarmingly over the last seven years. The program had a number of admirable qualities; while it was in no way the "revolution in news" promised in the promotion campaign, neither was it, as some had feared, the longest two hours in television. "NewsCenter 4" is a moderately well paced show. The hourly (ten-minute) and half-hourly (five-minute) news summaries alternating with specialized departments mean, theoretically, that "NewsCenter 4"—and viewers—won't suffer through slow news days; the features will take up the slack. In addition, the creators of "NewsCenter 4" offered Topic A—daily, five-minute "cover stories" or "backgrounders" to a major story in the news.

All in all, the program was a welcome break from the

fender benders, two-bit crimes, and smoky fires that for twenty years have been the predictable gruel of so much local television news. The first critical response was favorable. The *New York Times* television critic John O'Connor praised "NewsCenter 4" as "the most impressive thing to happen to local news in several years." *Variety*, the *Daily News*, and the *New York Post* were favorable too, and when the credits rolled after the first program, the usually sullen WNBC newsroom staff—like most TV news grunts, normally dyspeptic even when ratings are high—cheered like high-school kids.

Unfortunately, while Clive Barnes may make or break a new play on Broadway, most of the people who watch early evening television around New York don't read John O'Connor. And the people who might aren't at home at 5:00 or 6:00 P.M. watching television during the week. Not surprisingly, then, the Nielsen rating figures for the new NBC news told a different story from the reviews—or rather they told the same *old* story. "NewsCenter 4" earned a rating of 5 for the 6:00 to 7:00 P.M. "strip," which was its rating in the weeks before the premiere, and about the same circulation share—around a half-million viewers—that NBC had been getting for the past year. From 5:00 to 6:00, the ratings were *lower* than for the movies previously stripped in. By contrast, ABC's "Eyewitness News" was continuing to attract some 1.1 million viewers during May and CBS's "Six o'Clock Report" was staying at about 1.2 million viewers. Since the cost of a commercial minute on TV is determined mainly by audience size, the difference between NBC's ratings of 5 and CBS's and ABC's ratings of 10 and 11 could add up to $4 million to $5 million a year.

HE PROFIT MACHINES. . . . THE S

The Profit Machines

As these figures indicate, local news and local stations are important to the economic health of their proprietors. The owned-stations division of each network makes enormous contributions to the profits of the network. In 1970, for example, the 15 stations owned by ABC, CBS, and NBC together had revenues of $312 million (five VHF stations are the limit a network or broadcast group is allowed to own under FCC rules; by FCC practice, the networks can, perversely, report financial performance figures in a lump sum rather than by individual stations). Economically, 1970 was characterized by the FCC as a year of "stagnating revenues and rising costs." Nevertheless, the total reported profits for the 15 stations was $117 million, a very high percentage of revenue. Since 1970, both the revenue and the profit picture have been steadily brightening; in 1972, for example, the 15 owned stations had revenues of $327 million and profits of $102 million. The picture was even better for 1973 and 1974 (see pp. 90–91). By contrast, the major oil companies averaged profits of about 8.7 percent on revenues in 1973, according to a Chase Manhattan Bank survey. Indeed, operating a television station is more profitable than operating just about any other business, including network operations. In 1970, the three national networks collected revenues of $1.14 billion and reported profits of $50 million from their network operations (largely, the sale of time).

The sale of news times on local stations provides a significant percentage of local station revenues, which find their way to the networks directly in the case of owned stations. Local news, at both owned and affiliated sta-

DOCTORS . . . BETWEEN THE NECK

Broadcast Revenues, Expenses, and Income of Television Networks and Stations, 1972–1973 (in millions of dollars)

	1973	1972	% Increase 1972–1973
Broadcast revenues[1]			
3 networks	$1,404.9	$1,271.3	10.5
15 network owned-and-operated stations	353.1	327.1	7.9
All other stations			
474 VHF[2]	1,497.4	1,395.6	7.3
177 UHF[3]	209.4	185.4	12.9
Subtotal	1,706.8	1,581.1	7.9
INDUSTRY TOTAL	3,464.8	3,179.4	9.0
Broadcast expenses			
3 networks	$1,220.0	$1,160.4	5.1
15 networks owned-and-operated stations	250.3	224.6	11.4
All other stations			
474 VHF[2]	1,124.3	1,040.9	8.0
177 UHF[3]	217.0	201.4	7.7
Subtotal	1,341.4	1,242.3	8.0
INDUSTRY TOTAL	2,811.7	2,627.3	7.0
Broadcast income (before federal income tax)			
3 networks	$ 184.8	$ 110.9	66.6
15 network owned-and-operated stations	102.8	102.5	0.3
All other stations			
474 VHF[2]	373.1	354.7	5.2
177 UHF[3]	(7.7)	(15.9)	–
Subtotal	365.4	338.8	7.8
INDUSTRY TOTAL	653.1	552.2	18.3

[1] Net, after commissions to agencies, representatives, and brokers, after cash discounts.

[2] The 474 VHF stations represent 496 operations including 22 satellite stations that filed a combined report with their parent stations. The 1972 data reflect 475 VHF stations representing 493 operations including 18 satellites that filed a combined report with their parent stations.

[3] The 177 UHF stations represent 181 operations including 4 satellites that filed a combined report with their parent stations. The 1972 data reflect 173 UHF stations representing 182 operations including 9 satellites that filed a combined report with their parent stations.

Notes: Last digits may not add to totals because of rounding.
    ( ) denotes loss.

Source: Courtesy of *Broadcasting*, September 2, 1974.

AND THE KNEES . . . KICKERS, GU

**Broadcast Revenues (Gross) for 1973
and Projections for 1974**

	1973	1974
Network	$1,839,700,000	$2,045,000,000
Spot	1,230,200,000	1,290,000,000
Local	932,200,000	1,025,000,000
TOTAL	$4,002,100,000	$4,360,000,000

Source: Courtesy of Television Bureau of Advertising (TVB).

tions, also delivers something equally valuable—a large part of the audience for the network news. In many major markets, the local news comes on immediately before Cronkite, Chancellor, and Smith-Reasoner, providing a critical lead-in of audience. This new prominence has in recent years turned local stations into a battlefield for an intense, largely subterranean, struggle for the control of the news. The struggle has nothing to do with the White House, the FCC, the advertisers, or any of the better-known news managers. It is, rather, a contention between the journalists and the audience researchers, between—permit me—Art and Science. To the extent that the "scientists" prevail, the opportunities for serious local news content will be further diminished.

The Show Doctors
Up until a few years ago, television news was in the hands of professional news directors and producers, traditionally trained in newspaper or magazine work or broadcast journalism. It still is, at the networks. But local station management has not had the same professional approach,

RGASMS—AND OTHER REMEDIES

especially since the local stations began discovering that
their news times could be highly salable, often cheaper
to run than straight entertainment shows, and attractive
to many advertisers. Not only has television news become
longer, from 15 or 30 minutes of headlines-weather-sports
to 60 and 90 and 120 minutes of heavily orchestrated
production; in many stations, television news has become
too important to be left to the newspeople. Audience
research has been perceived as the key to ratings success.

At the networks and the broadcast chains, the researchers are usually staff social scientists working with outside
hired consultants. Typically, they conduct surveys of
audience demography and make continuing samplings of
specific viewer reactions. NBC in New York has gone in
heavily for audience surveys—"the most comprehensive
and expensive research operation in the history of the
world," NBC News Vice-President Lee Hanna once told
his staff. Usually, the lower the ratings, the greater the
use of the survey researchers. Emmanuel "Manny"
Demby, the audience consultant for "NewsCenter 4,"
has been using a questionnaire technique he calls
"psychographics" to get at the connection, if any, between the personalities of viewers and elements of the
news. Demby often uses a "test facility"—a tastefully
furnished room at the offices of Demby's Motivational
Programmers, Inc., at 770 Lexington Avenue in New
York. There, Demby and his NBC clients can observe,
through one-way glass, a roomful of unsuspecting people
as they watch "NewsCenter 4."

At smaller stations, on the other hand, the only researchers and pulse takers are almost always outside consultants; most of them have minimal news experience.

..."SAVING" CHANNEL 4: A CASE

They are show doctors, and their fever charts are the ratings. All around the country, they have become final arbiters of the news, from the length of film stories to the qualifications of the on-air talent. Among their most consistent prescriptions are large doses of "personal news." This RX has been particularly murderous as far as politics and national affairs—the "public news"—are concerned.

The consultants read the printouts and tell their station-patients that most viewers are more interested in local news than national news most of the time (wars and other extraordinary events are the obvious exceptions, but not, in the consultants' experience, over extended periods of time). Were it not for the local news lead-in, millions of people, it is said, might skip the national news entirely. Viewers, so the consultants' reasoning goes, care about *their* weather tomorrow, *their* home team scores, *their* roads, hospitals, and public services (when they are affected by repairs or strikes), the cost of *their* subway or bus fares, the pollution at *their* beaches. The consultants' unwritten constitution of "self-evident truths" about viewers has produced a hierarchy of news values that goes something like this, in ascending order of interest:

— European and British news ranks higher than African/Asian/Latin American news (except when American military operations or American nationals are involved).

— Washington political news and national news rank higher than European news.

— National disasters on a large scale are more important than Washington political news.

rORY ... DISCOVERING "WARMT

— Local disasters are more important than national disasters.

— Local sports, local weather, and other such "personal news" are most important of all.

. . . Between the Neck and the Knees

These rules, of course, are not ironclad. Nor were they, in all fairness, discovered only recently by the television consultants. Seventy years of Anglo-American journalism have demonstrated that the "personal news" that usually excites the most avid interest centers on accounts of sex and violence—hence the tabloid axiom: "Keep it between the neck and the knees. . . ." But even the more "serious" news outlets stress the personal. Newspaper and wire service reporters quite early in their professional lives absorb the rough rule of thumb that, in terms of reader interest, "10,000 deaths in Nepal equals 100 deaths in Wales equals 10 deaths in West Virginia equals one death next door." In recent years, with the increased social and political sensitivity of news directors, such rules have been muted a bit. But they still operate, and in the best places. In the *Washington Post* one morning a few years ago, the prominent story and accompanying picture of the crash in an airline disaster that killed 70 members of a football team from nearby West Virginia appeared "above the fold" (the top half of the front page). Below the fold, in the bottom left corner, was a wire service account of typhoons that had killed "tens of thousands of villagers" in Sri Lanka. More recently, during the month of February 1974, the records of the Television News Archive at Vanderbilt University, where all three network newscasts are videotape-recorded and indexed,

" . . . NEWS VERSUS "NEWSZAK"

show no news on film at all from Rome for any of the
networks and only one film story from Tokyo. Did
nothing happen in Italy or Japan during the month?
Not at all. More accurately, nothing happened in Italy or
Japan that, in the near-unanimous opinion of the network news producers, could "compete" with such domestic stories as Watergate, the energy "crisis," and the
Patricia Hearst kidnapping.

Kickers, Guts, Orgasms—and Other Remedies
Broadcasters offer all sorts of reasons for bringing in the
computers and the consultants: they help serve the viewers better, they identify community needs, they tell
advertisers who is watching and why. But audience
research exists first and last because, almost without
exception, station management wants the highest possible ratings for its news times. The television consultants
thrive on the not unreasonable theory that the management of any given broadcast chain or station is usually
(1) too close to the daily operations to see why there
are rating shortfalls (if that is the case) and/or (2) too
protective of its own interests to change anything ("How
could it be wrong if we did it?"). Once invited in to look
over news and public affairs programming, the consultant's work usually follows a familiar pattern: conferences with the station management; quantitative studies
of the market, including random sampling of a cross section of the viewers (400 interviews on the average);
analysis and interpretation of the figures, together with
recommendations for on-air changes in the news.

There are, however, wide differences in the ways these
steps are carried out by the various firms. The cost of

these services also varies—from $10,000 to $50,000 or more, plus follow-up fees, depending on the size of the market. As of mid-1974, two consulting firms were most active in refurbishing the news on television, while a number of smaller companies shared what business was left over.

McHugh and Hoffman, Inc., of McLean, Virginia, was one of the Big Two. The oldest of the television broadcast consultants, McHugh and Hoffman, Inc., was founded by two graduates of the Campbell Ewald advertising agency in 1962. Its earliest rating success came with the ABC-owned and operated stations in New York, Los Angeles, and Chicago. ABC News also used McHugh and Hoffman to find out who watches the network news and why. The firm's most recent big winner is the "Tabloid TV" format at KGO, San Francisco. KGO in two years moved from indifferent ratings numbers to a 45 percent average share of the audience. The station featured so many sex items, murders, nudity stories, rapes, violent crimes, and (allegedly) humorous "punch line" stories that CBS News correspondent Mike Wallace once said the call letters stood for "Kickers, Guts, Orgasms." In 1974, the McHugh and Hoffman product could be seen at some 30 client stations. They are often tagged "Eyewitness News" (or "The Scene Tonight") and are immediately recognizable by the upbeat musical introduction, the blazers, the panning camera, the "newsteam" (three or more people sitting at airlines-style reservation counter desks), and the emphasis on establishing "rapport." "The anchorman is someone who is asking the audience to invite him into their homes," a McHugh-Hoffman report to a client states; "it takes a very special kind of personality. . . ."

Frank N. Magid Associates, of Marion, Iowa, was the largest of the consultant firms. In 1974, Magid claimed some 85 broadcast clients. The founder was formerly a professor of sociology at the University of Iowa and Coe College before going into the audience and news research business. In one of the most successful resuscitations performed by a show doctor, Magid helped raise Philadelphia's WPVI (a Capital Cities station) from number three in the ratings to number one in a year. His formula was the "Action News" approach: 30 to 40 short, fast items in 22 minutes or so, "one-minute-thirty for World War III," a rival says. Also Magid likes movement on camera— "a cast of thousands." Magid performed his miracle in Philadelphia partly on the basis of a survey showing "what the people said it liked and disliked. . . ." Some typical Magid recommendations, according to a study by Edward Barrett, former dean of the Columbia University Graduate School of Journalism, call for "simplifying and limiting treatment of complex news and elimination of 'upper-class' English," among other measures.[2]

Melvin A. Goldberg, Inc., Communications, of New York, is considerably smaller than the Magid or McHugh-Hoffman operations. A five-year-old firm, its letterhead forms the acronym MAGI*C—much to the irritation of Frank Magid. Goldberg is a 1950 graduate of Columbia University, where he studied with Paul Lazarsfeld. Goldberg's modest list of clients includes WTOP-TV, the Post-Newsweek station in Washington, and Westinghouse's KWY-TV in Philadelphia. Since Magid has WPVI, Philadelphia's Action News station, the two men were in a head-to-head battle of the consultants. Goldberg told me that he has a "nonformula formula . . . something distinct for each market." Goldberg makes particular use of group interviews—ten people "interacting" for about 90 minutes—in order to find out the *why* of viewing (Goldberg's answer: "It's a psychological thing; there are other motivations for watching TV than to be informed. . . . They want reassurance, for one thing. . . ."

Rierson Broadcast Consultants, of New York, is another small operation. Robert Rierson describes his company as "a full-service consultancy in news."[3] Some of his competitors, he says, "have no actual station experience." Rierson has worked for stations in Charlotte, North Carolina, Washington, and New York (Channel 2). "These other consultants," he says, "do a market survey with some questionnaires and plop the results on the desk of the station manager. We have staff specialists who can come into newsrooms and tell them that 'the flow is wrong' or 'the set is wrong,' and what to do about it. . . . Of course they have to be good at human relations. . . ." Rierson and his partner, Barbara Reisenbach (who used to work for Nielsen), claim a dozen or so full-service clients and another dozen clients who get specialized services. His philosophy in revamping the news is that "good journalism isn't alienated from show business techniques."

Motivational Programmers, Inc., of New York is Dr. Emmanuel Demby's firm, now working with NBC's own staff researchers for "NewsCenter 4." One of MPI's distinct services is studying group interactions in "a homelike atmosphere." Demby's discussion groups, usually about twelve people grouped around a television set, are asked to describe the program they are watching and to rate the talent and the news items. Demby's confidential reports to management discuss newspeople in terms of their "contributions" to the program. He then may make "recommendations on what could be done to maximize their appeal. . . ."

While NBC and ABC News have become converts to the practice of using consultants, CBS says it remains unconvinced; according to CBS News President Richard Salant, "We can't be motivated in the news by what people want as opposed to what they need if they are to be reasonably informed."[4] Mel Bernstein, the news director of WNAC-TV in Boston, is another skeptic; Bernstein says WNAC was told by its consultant, Frank Magid, to deemphasize political coverage on grounds of viewer unconcern. But Bernstein chose not to follow the recommendation, citing his own opinion that Boston "is one of the most politically oriented cities in the country." Another critical opinion of the consultants was offered by Richard Townley, a television news director in Tulsa, Oklahoma; he concluded that since there are few truly original ideas around, the consultant merely collects successful ideas in an organized way, suggesting features and gimmicks that can "hype" the ratings and are transferable from one city to another.[5] Nonjournalists have been critical, too; Professor David J. LeRoy of Florida State University reports that in analyzing one Magid audience survey, he found a questionable sample size, "biased" language, and inconsistent tabulations. Edward Barrett suspects that "many or most of the consultants' recommendations would have been the same had there been no survey."

Once a consultant "upgrades" the news, it would seem to be a permanent fix, like expensive orthodontics. I once asked Goldberg if his business wouldn't self-destruct eventually. "No," he replied. "It is self-perpetuating. Another guy comes in and fixes the opposition and your client needs help again. . . ."

"Saving" Channel 4: A Case History

NBC News was very tardy in getting into this new cult of extensive head counting and pulse taking. It didn't believe in research as long as it was number one, both nationally and in New York during most of the middle and late 1960s, with its distinct, Olympian style of news. "We were preserved, like a fly in amber," Wald now says. Meanwhile, ABC and CBS in New York began loosening up the old forms of the news. ABC's "Eyewitness News" was in part a product of audience survey research showing that viewers wanted "warmth" and "involvement" on the screen—"People reporting to other people," in the phase of ABC's Al Primo, the chief in-house architect of the "Eyewitness News" approach. As NBC New York's ratings plummeted—at one point it was registering an asterisk (*) in the weekly rating books, meaning its audience was so small it couldn't be measured—a taxi squad of news directors and executive producers shuttled in and out of Rockefeller Center. Each new regime would fuss with format, changing anchormen, or increasing the promotion budgets, or hiring new reporters, or altering the set, or switching sportscasters, or redoing the graphics, or renaming the program. Literally millions of dollars were spent, but very little went into the basics of the news—filming, writing, and reporting.

NBC shouldn't be singled out for its desperate scramblings; at CBS's owned station in New York, WCBS, the ratings were good, if not overwhelming, during the same period; still, the station felt compelled to shift around the furnishings of the news periodically. WCBS, according to an internal memo obtained by journalists Ron Powers and Jerrold Oppenheim,[6] made annual expenditures for such show business touches as:

Two new sets for each of the last two years	$100,000
Anchorman Jim Jensen's salary	150,000
A newly added anchorman's salary	60,000
An announcer to say, "Here is Jim Jensen"	17,500
A fourth camera for an opening "beauty shot" from above (permanently mounted, and with no other use), including maintenance	52,000

It was enough to give journalism a bad name.

Discovering "Warmth"

The researchers' major "finding" of the 1970s is that people don't want their news to be dull. This information has been treated like the epochal discovery of Copernicus; thanks to science, programs no longer revolve around one Great Stone Face. But many critics suspected that for years. NBC News's 1960s success, Huntley and Brinkley, owed its ratings as much to the chemistry between the two men (Huntley-Brinkley, Huntley-Brinkley/One is solemn, the other twinkly) as to its information value; this interplay masked the rigidity of the anchorman–film report–anchorman form. When Lee Hanna was in charge of the Channel 2 news a few years back, he brought in a platoon of specialists and local reporters and gained ratings points. Al Primo's informal, more human "Eye-witness News" team also attracted viewers at an astonishing rate—again at the expense of NBC. CBS countered by warming up its image still more. Walter Cronkite on the network news may still be neatly buttoned in his Finchley suit, but WCBS's Dave Marash appears in New York with a beard, short sleeves, and a cigar stuck in his mouth. NBC's "NewsCenter 4" completes the demolition of the old-style news; the program design and the advertising promotion urge people to tune in on specific features—what the researchers call "audience interest segments"—such as Lifestyle (5:14) or Newsdesk (6:01) or Topic A, "Our Daily Cover Story" (6:50), rather than tuning in on The Cronkite or The Chancellor.

With "NewsCenter 4," NBC News in New York has changed *everything* at once—format, set, graphics, on-air staff, even its advertising promotion agency. While the boldest change, the increase from one to two hours, was the idea of the journalists of NBC, "the research" played a critical part in, first, the decision-making process and, second, the program itself.

———

In addition to circulation troubles from 6:00 to 7:00 in New York, WNBC's 4:30 to 6:00 P.M. nightly strip had become increasingly difficult to program. Motion pictures are a usual solution for the late afternoon audience; but NBC's motion-picture properties have long been weak. Off-network serials—former prime-time shows available for syndication—are another late afternoon possibility, and for a time, some of the NBC sales people argued against expanding the news and for a "Marcus Welby, M.D." package due on the market in 1975. In the end, research figures decisively demonstrated that an audience was available for news.

One study mirrored the success of NBC's two-hour news in Los Angeles, but since Los Angeles is an 8:30 to

4:00 working town, where television news viewing takes the place of an afternoon newspaper, the figures weren't very influential. More important was research by NBC's own audience specialist, William Rubens, indicating that 75 percent of the New York audience watching the news at 6:00 P.M. is also available to watch at 5:00. Audience flow studies suggested one group of viewers—largely, the over-fifty crowd—would stay with a program through the whole two hours, while another, larger—and younger—group would join it at various points in progress. Other research confirmed that the late afternoon New York television audience tended to be female, blue-collar, and older (NBC found that its ratings trailed off even more than usual on Fridays—"when our older Jews go to syna-gogue," Hanna suggests).

Rubens and Demby also helped in NBC's search for on-air personalities. In all, NBC videotape-recorded the news programs of every station in the Top Forty markets —over 125 stations at $200 a station for the videotape alone. Lee Hanna and his news director, Earl Ubell, screened all the tapes personally. From a group of four-teen semifinalists, NBC picked about six anchorman candidates, taking into account their reporting ability, camera presence, and contract availability. Rubens and Demby ran a series of experiments to test the public response to the talent. Interviewers in special vans, much like the tuberculosis society's x-ray units, parked at sub-urban shopping centers and enticed passersby inside to watch a few minutes of tapes; people in the sample were then asked to explain why they preferred one anchor-person to another. In addition, viewers were brought to Rockefeller Center and paid to watch tapes and vote their choices. A pilot tape of the new program was tested on cable television systems in New Jersey and on Long Island; tapes were shown at a theater in California where the seats are fitted with levers to register audience reaction (and where viewers wouldn't recognize New York faces). Phone interviews and written questionnaires followed up the tests. One outside consultant estimates that NBC probably spent $100,000 on the research for this phase alone.

Like so much current social science research, the NBC testing operation told Wald, Hanna, and Ubell a great deal of what they already knew. Dr. Frank Field with science-medicine stories and Betty Furness's consumer action segments placed highest in viewer preference. Carl Stokes, the onetime mayor of Cleveland, also scored high with "Urban Journal," street reporting that took him out of the studio; two years before, when Stokes was cast with a reporter named Paul Udell as coanchorman, NBC News hit one of its lowest circulation points. The tests eventually validated two of the NBC brass's preferences for the three jobs as program hosts: Jim Hartz, thirty-three, a steady, capable newsman who had been with the station for ten years, and Chuck Scarborough, thirty, a cool Robert Redford type. Hartz, according to one research report, "is liked but he is not the most liked" of New York anchorpeople. Scarborough, the tests showed, had "great woman appeal."

Hartz and Scarborough together were being paid over $250,000 a year; in 1968, Scarborough had been working out of the Biloxi, Mississippi, hotel lobby studio of station WLOX, earning about $18,000 a year. In the last few years, as researchers and consultants have exchanged tapes of on-air people as if they were trading cards, the price of the talent has, in Hanna's words, "escalated beyond belief. . . ."

The third man chosen was Jim Van Sickle, a solid, fiftyish broadcaster. For the first three weeks, Van Sickle did "NewsCenter 4" hourly and half-hourly hard news summaries, which meant that he had more air time than the two stars together. After the first ratings came out—and the first research, indicating Van Sickle "wasn't very memorable"—Van Sickle was sent on an assignment to Israel. Hartz started doing the news summaries to get maximum exposure. There was no hurry to get Van Sickle back; when the Israeli-Syrian front quieted, he was sent to Ireland. Eventually, he was assigned to street reporting.

Two months after the program had started, the star, Hartz, himself left to move up to the coveted job of co-host of NBC's "Today Show." The entire elaborate, and expensive, talent search and testing that had produced the Hartz-Scarborough team had to begin again, somewhat grimly. Since Scarborough was new to New York, his "recognition factor" was low. Another anchor personality with "low recognition," so the reasoning went, would place an intolerable burden on a new program. In late fall, Tom Snyder, a Los Angeles broadcaster who had received some national exposure as the host of NBC's "Tomorrow Show," was given the assignment.

"NewsCenter 4" was conceived as the television of the 1970s. The central figure of the anchorman was to be muted. The emphasis instead was to be on the program's feature departments, or what the audience researchers chose to call "the interest segments." According to Wald, they resemble a "news magazine way of doing things, well suited to television."

News versus "Newszak"

Actually, the true model is not print at all. The real parent of "NewsCenter 4" is the "Today Show," moved to the early evening hours, news packages alternating with features and interviews. And the parentage of the "Today Show," in turn, is radio. No one has to watch Barbara Walters and company; listening is enough as you wake, dress, and feed the cat (according to Bill Monroe, the respected editor who until early 1975 did the "Today Show" Washington interviews, "Many people say that all they have to do is sample the guest to 'fix' him in their minds, and they leave the room"). NBC's research—again confirming common sense—shows that the same thing happens in the early evening.

Is the new-style news of the seventies, then, nothing more than background sound, a kind of "Newszak"? Does that represent "progress" from the print era? The "Today Show" succeeds—its audience of 7 million is five times the size of the audience attracted by the competing "CBS Morning News"—not just because of a convenient format but because of content as well: it is a good show. It achieved acceptance without any of the ministrations of the audience researchers. "If [the executive producer Stuart] Schulberg is interested in something—a book, a person or an issue," says an associate, "then he assumes that other people should be, too. He wants it on." In short, this approach has been the characteristic that successful newspaper and magazine proprietors have in common, too.

It is always tempting—and too easy—to romanticize about such good old seat-of-the-pants journalism. The mumbo jumbo of the marketing men is an easy-to-hit dartboard. Clearly, the researchers' information ought to supplement the journalists' experience; just as clearly, a news program can't be put together based on "the research." Research can tell news editors what the audience is thinking; it can't devise any formula for what news ought to be covered. The NBC attempt to combine art and measurement makes sense—in the abstract. It is, as usual, the execution that counts. If gimmickry is all that is needed to attract—and keep—the New York television audience, then stations could go the route of the latest ratings sensation, the crime–sex–traffic accident, story-every-30-seconds "Action News" format—the Tabloid Television style pushed by the show doctors and consultants.

They could raise the ratings; it would be no problem— as someone once said—but it would be wrong. There is a better way. "NewsCenter 4" was conceived as quality television; its creators set their goals higher than at any other station in the country. At the planning sessions for the Topic A features—"our cover stories"—such weighty subjects as "NATO at 25," "The Housewife and Inflation," and "Gun Control" were blocked out. In practice, Topic A stories have tended toward "higher viewer interest" fluff like massage parlors in New York City and wild dog packs on Long Island. At great expense, NBC's executives collected what they judged was an excellent staff of newspeople—and then kept commissioning surveys to see if the audience had "accepted" their judgment. Like an erratic tennis player, NBC kept looking

around—behind, to the side, above, below—everyplace
but where the good player is supposed to keep his eye—
on the ball, on the news.

The audience surveys can help; the ups and downs of
the circulation competition can provide a rough measure
of effectiveness. But when either the research or the
ratings take over the direction of the news, it is no longer
journalism—no matter how "newsy" the surroundings or
how many bodies are on the screen or what the program
is called. This, as it turned out, is what happened when
the ABC network created "A.M. America" as an early
morning rival to the "Today Show." "A.M. America" was
introduced in January 1975, after more than two years
of planning. The "warm" colors of the sets, the tempo of
the music, and the "chemistry" of the hosts, Stephanie
Edwards and Bill Beutel, were all products of surveys conducted by Frank Magid. The show doctors claimed that
they had found younger nonviewers who could be lured
into turning on their sets in the morning by a fast-moving
format. On "A.M. America," the news is delivered in bursts
of information, like the commercials on television. The
result was a form of information that tends to be weak—
morning coffee with too much sugar and cream. The
audience confounded Magid by avoiding the program.

Still, as long as revenues—and prestige—are directly tied
to the ratings, both local stations and the national networks will continue to worry over such strategies and will
continue to call in the consultants. They often affect
only the surface appearance of the news. These marginal
competitive considerations may signify merely that one
or another network may make a few more megabucks or
that some unlucky news executive will end up teaching

broadcast journalism somewhere. More important, there is also the matter of what the viewer gets in the *content* of the public news. In the next section, specific examples of coverage of major events of the 1960s and early 1970s are discussed. In some cases, as much, if not more, material is presented from newspapers and magazines as from television news. There is no evidence, however, that the performance of television news differed significantly from the performance of the print news examples cited.

Part II

THE CONTENT OF THE PUBLIC NEWS

Chapter 6
Vietnam: Who Was the Enemy?

I don't know much and come to think about it, what I do know ain't so.

—An American speaking in *The People, Yes,* by Carl Sandburg

The words above are quoted by Douglas Pike in his study *Viet Cong: The Organization and Techniques of the National Liberation Front of South Vietnam.* Pike, a foreign service officer with the United States Information Agency, was a supporter of the American intervention in Vietnam. He observes that "For Americans Vietnam has grown steadily as a crisis in perception, one that began with a failure in definition. It is both symbolic and significant that no appellation coined for the opposing insurgent forces was acceptable to all parties, including the insurgents themselves. In this sense they were never defined."

This is an astonishing statement. In all the megatonnage of commentary unleashed about the media's role in covering Vietnam, not much has been said about the terms that American newspapers, magazines, and broadcasters used to describe the combatants. To suggest that the American media didn't even know who the "enemy" was or what to call him is a staggering thought. One of the first reporting principles that young journalists used to be taught was to get the name and address right; if the story garbled these facts, then the reader couldn't be expected to have much confidence in the rest of the account.

In order to learn more about the "language" of the Vietnam coverage and the media's "crisis of perception," I looked into a heavy sampling of reportage over the last 24 years of American involvement in Indochina. Working with me was Jane Pratt, who speaks and reads Vietnamese. Ms. Pratt had spent considerable time in Saigon from 1963 to 1969 and had finished her Ph.D. work in the Department of Political Science at MIT in 1970. We wanted to find out how the media described the "other side" in Vietnam. Our work began as a deliberately modest exercise. There have been enough broad-canvas studies of the United States and Vietnam. As a framework, we divided the American press's coverage into the five generally accepted phases of American involvement.

The first phase, the era of benign ignorance, lasted from, roughly, the end of the Second World War to about 1961. During this period, Vietnam and Indochina were considered to be outside the sphere of America's Asiatic interests. Few American journalists had visited Indochina; practically none knew the language or customs. I can, in fact, recall my own experience as an intelligence officer during the Korean War; the Indochina "section" of the key American military intelligence-gathering service didn't even own a bound Vietnamese-language dictionary. Coverage of Vietnam in the American press was minimal through the 1950s; with the possible exception of the fall of Dien Bien Phu, Indochina hardly penetrated the American consciousness between 1946 and 1960.

Second came a period of gradual military buildup, from 1961 to 1965. As the Kennedy Administration, and later the Johnson Administration, began introducing U.S. ground troops, Vietnam became an American "story." The story in some cases was being covered from Hong Kong—where the national news organizations maintained a

ENTER THE CONG . . . PHASING O

Mid-Asian watch (pleasant living and English spoken)—or from Saigon by French-born journalists, such as the late François Sully of *Newsweek*. A number of younger American reporters also were assigned to Vietnam. Few, if any, knew the Vietnamese language or history; many did not even speak French. They tended to be young males in their twenties, relatively inexperienced and almost completely on their own. Journalists are often eager for combat; junior reporters win their stripes in the field, just as the Army's junior officers do. Young men can take the physical side of war reportage better than older men and—not so incidentally—don't cost as much to maintain in the field. Gloria Emerson, who was stationed in Saigon as a *New York Times* correspondent, refers to some of these younger men as "the Easy Riders," bent on making their reputations through the war story.[1]

During this period of gradual buildup, American reporters almost uniformly supported the U.S. commitment. They were "on the team." They did not question the officially stated policy of "containing" communism and thus preventing the Chinese "takeover" of Indochina. The press held to the principle of the domino theory, while quarreling here and there with the execution of the American commitment (for example, with the Saigon government's treatment of the Buddhist factions).

The third period of press coverage began in 1965 with the introduction of large-unit American ground forces by the Johnson Administration. The American media also stepped up their commitment to coverage; at the high point of American involvement in Vietnam, no fewer than 550 to 650 men and women were accredited to the U.S. Military Assistance Command in Vietnam (MACV). This

E "REDS" . . . "LET'S SAY IT RIGH

was the time of the "Five o'Clock Follies"—the daily briefings for correspondents in Saigon. It was also the time of what the perceptive critic Michael Arlen called the "Living Room War." Between 1965 and 1968 the Americans and the North Vietnamese engaged in several large-unit battles. Thanks to technology and the freedom that MACV gave correspondents, the three American networks were able to send camera crews by helicopter into the fighting, film the battle scenes, speed the footage back to Saigon, and airlift it to Hong Kong, Bangkok, or Tokyo, where it was beamed via satellite to some 47 million American television viewers each evening. A generation of television watchers had certain images firmly fixed in its mind's eye: the Cobra gunships swooping in; the firefights along the highways; bent little old men (Were they farmers, or were they the "enemy"?) in rice paddies; families huddled around thatched-roof huts; close-in bomb strikes; and every once in a while an elusive figure running toward the treeline as tracers explode around him. This was television's period of "shooting bloody"—getting the battle scenes on film.

The North Vietnamese–National Liberation Front "Tet" offensive of January–March 1968 signaled a fourth stage in the war. Tet has been called the "high point of military action in the Second Indochina War, and, in all likelihood, the only battle of the war anyone will long remember."[2] The plan of action called for a simultaneous surprise attack on nearly every city, town, and major military base throughout South Vietnam. It was audacious, it was spectacular—and it was costly to the enemy. The American General William Westmoreland could declare that Tet was a great military setback for the enemy; in terms of men

T!" . . . ICONOGRAPHY OF THE W

killed and equipment lost, the Tet offensive probably was a "defeat" for the North and Front forces. But the impact of Tet on the American public was, it was said, a "psychological" victory for the other side. The pressures to end American involvement grew.

With the election of Nixon in 1968, the fifth act of the Vietnam "story" began. The Nixon Administration widened the war—invading Cambodia in 1970 and Laos in 1971—in order to "wind it down." The winding-down, the removal of American ground combat troops, took until 1972.

Enter the Cong
Most historians and analysts now agree that, at the time of the Geneva accords "ending" the First (French) Indochina War in 1954, there were south of the 17th parallel in Vietnam thousands of Northerners, Southerners, Communists, Resistance fighters, socialists, religious factionalists, and nationalists. These widely varied dissidents opposed the French- and American-supported government in Saigon. As early as 1956, Saigon newspapers began referring to these diverse groups as Vietcong; the term "Cong" is an abbreviation for "Cong-san," meaning Communist. The antigovernment groups surfaced in 1960 and chose as their name the National Liberation Front of South Vietnam. The NLF didn't like the term "Vietcong." They thought it was, as one NLF official said at the time, "a contemptuous appellation which lumps together Communists and others." But the name caught on.

Anyone reading the political and social history of Vietnam prior to the NLF's emergence becomes extraordinarily sensitive to the nuances of such matters—in hindsight. Few, if any, of the distinctions are conveyed in the

WINDING DOWN THE COVERAGE

stories or broadcast reports. Even the *New York Times,* journal of record and the American paper with the most extensive foreign coverage, relied on the shorthand of journalese. On November 11, 1960, for example, the *Times* carried a story with the headline COUP AGAINST DIEM. Here are some excerpts:

> The U.S. has strongly supported Ngo Dinh Diem in his campaign against the Communists. . . .
> The revolt came after weeks of unrest in the pro-Western nation as a result of increased Communist subversion. . . . The North Vietnam Communists have sent more and more agents into the area in an effort to overthrow their implacable foe. . . .
> North Vietnam is Red-ruled under the leadership of Ho Chi Minh. . . .
> In a recent clash forty-one members of the Communist forces and thirteen South Vietnamese soldiers were killed. . . .

By 1963, the process of "reductionism" was producing some unintended humor. One Washington correspondent referred to the "Communist guerrillas of the Vietcong"; another broadcaster called the National Liberation Front the "political arm of the Vietcong," which was something like saying the "Republican Party is the political arm of the Republican Party." Repeatedly, there seemed to be a need for overkill: it wasn't enough to call the enemy "insurgents" or "guerrillas"; they must be called "Communist insurgents" *(Los Angeles Times,* August 14, 1966) or "Vietcong guerrillas" *(New York Times,* January 1, 1966). The usage "National Liberation Front" was rare, and when it did occur, it usually was in the form "Communist National Liberation Front" (Crosby Noyes, *Washington Star,* August 13, 1966).

By the mid-sixties, the media had fixed on four or five designations for the other side: "Communist guerrillas," "Vietcong raiders," "Hanoi's forces," "Communists," and—in headlines and wire copy—"Reds." Parenthetical translations of "Vietcong" no longer appeared. The designations "NLF" and "Front" seldom appeared in the U.S. press; they were, however, common style in, for example, the French newspaper *Le Monde*.

Phasing Out the "Reds"

Beginning in 1966–1967, another shift in terms occurred. The words "Communists" and "Reds" started to fade away in stories. The preferred phrases were "Vietcong" and "North Vietnamese troops." These changes were related to a number of factors. First, of course, regular battalions of North Vietnamese had entered the fighting. But there was also a growing antiwar sentiment in the United States which was forcing some of the more thoughtful correspondents to go back to first assumptions. R. W. Apple, Jr., of the *New York Times* recalls that when he was bureau chief in Saigon he forbade his staff to use the term "Communist" except when referring to the North Vietnamese forces. Apple says he was acutely conscious of the problems of terminology and vetoed the word "Communist" out of a belief that "there were substantial non-Communist elements in the Vietcong and therefore the term was misleading. . . ."[3]

There was, however, an unintended irony in Apple's decision. In the period 1960–1966, when the media had papered the Red label over all of the opposition forces fighting in South Vietnam, there were still significant non-Communist elements in that opposition; but by the middle and late 1960s, when the new sophistication took over and the word "Communist" was shelved, the opposition really *was* largely Communist. The war had entered its large-unit battle phase, and American firepower had severely reduced the ranks of the original NLF forces, which had included a diversity of backgrounds. The North Vietnamese regulars had taken their places.

By 1968, the usage "Vietcong and North Vietnamese" seemed to be the preferred formulation, except when brevity was wanted. Not everyone was pleased with these usages, though. In June 1968, Roger Tatarian, vice-president and editor of United Press International, received a letter from an editor questioning use of the phrases "Communist troop concentrations" and "Communist armor." Tatarian, in *UPI Reporter,* conceded that "these are fair questions." He explained:

When it is possible to say with accuracy that the opposing forces are Vietcong or North Vietnamese, we so specify. When it is not, we often use the broader term of "communist." . . . Why do we not simply refer to the other side in Vietnam as the "enemy" or the "foe"? Because we are an international news agency. . . . For the UPI to speak of "enemy" forces would hardly establish its objectivity in the eyes of the people who were not involved. And if technical considerations are not important, it should also be kept in mind that the United States is not in a formal state of war and that the word "enemy" would therefore not be any great technical improvement.

An examination of the major publications and network news transcripts in the United States reveals the same general patterns: early use of "Hanoi" and "Communists" as catchall terms, a shift to "Vietcong," then to "Vietcong and North Vietnamese," and finally to "enemy." By early 1970, most of the media had all but jettisoned the terms "Communists" and "Reds."

Then came the invasion of Cambodia—and the American media saw Red once more. On May 1, 1970, the *New York Times* reported that President Nixon had sent combat forces into Cambodia "to drive the Communists from strategic areas" and to "eliminate a major Communist staging area." Like a recurrent bad dream, the process began again. U.S. troops, South Vietnamese troops, and "our" Cambodians fought against the "Vietcong" or "North Vietnamese." The possibility that there might be Cambodians on the other side seldom came up in the news accounts.

The Cambodian leader, Prince Sihanouk, called his government-in-exile Front Uni de la Nation Khmer, or FUNK; in English this becomes the Cambodian National Front. The Communist Party in Cambodia is known as the Khmer Rouge. If these usages sound unfamiliar, they should. They were not commonly employed in the U.S. media—with two notable exceptions. Richard Dudman of the *St. Louis Post-Dispatch* and Robert Anson of *Time* magazine were captured separately during the Cambodian fighting. After they were released, both wrote long and absorbing accounts of their time on the other side. And both managed to write about their captors without using the adjectives "Communist" or "Red" or the noun "enemy." Dudman's story contains such usages as "Cambodian and Vietnamese guerrillas," "guerrilla troops supporting Norodom Sihanouk," "a North Vietnamese commander," and "a local Cambodian commander."[4]

In *Time,* the editors who prepared the introduction to Anson's account took extra care with their words, writing that Anson was captured "by anti-government forces." No doubt, some of this circumspection was due to the fact that other American journalists were still missing and presumed captured, and no one wanted to jeopardize their chances. Yet the evident care given to designations by both Dudman and Anson creates an entirely different tone in their articles. Their care also increased the reader's understanding of the forces involved in Cambodia, and that, after all, is what good journalism is supposed to do. So the question arises: Why wasn't this same craftsmanlike care shown from the very beginning of the American coverage of Vietnam?

"Let's Say It Right!"

A decade ago, one answer might be that using nonpejorative terms like "Front" or "Revolutionaries" would have seemed too much like being "soft" on communism. We all have paid in many ways for such habits. Perhaps as long as the other side could be seen as the hated, depersonalized "Reds" and "Communists"—rather than through Dudman's and Anson's perception of them as "young men" or "soldiers"—then it became easier to absorb the "enemy body count" nightly on the TV news. This explanation assumes that someone made a conscious decision about what names should be used. It is true that, much later in the war, the U.S. Military Assistance Command in Vietnam issued a directive to the military Armed Forces radio service in Vietnam (AFVN). "Let's Say It Right," the memo instructed, and listed a variety of "correct" and "incorrect" terms, including:

Incorrect	Correct
VC Tax Collectors	VC Extortionists
Peoples Liberation Army	Viet Cong (or if appropriate, North Vietnamese Army—NVA)

Incorrect	*Correct*
National Liberation Front	Viet Cong
Five o'Clock Follies	MACV Daily Briefings (or Daily Press Briefings)

In the early and mid-1960s, however, the "free" press corps picked up and reflexively used the officially correct terms largely because it had no confident independent knowledge of the Vietnamese language or of Vietnamese internal politics.

Iconography of the War

The inability to find a proper name for the enemy was not, as I said, one of the "big" themes of the Vietnam War; neither is it a minor matter. In many ways, it was a war of words and images. The *iconography* of Vietnam—how it was pictured—helped determine the direction of American policy. The most succinct summing-up of the 15-year American involvement in Indochina that I know was made by the Harvard economist Wassily Leontief. Other critics have taken whole volumes to say what he compresses into one sentence:

A naive simplistic view of the internal social struggles shaping the emergence of a small Asiatic country from its colonial past caused the United States to pay a colossal price in treasure, human lives and immoral standing throughout the civilized world. [5]

The iconography of the "Communist" enemy was one part of the naive simplistic view of the time, but hardly the only one. The notorious phrases "protective reaction," "Vietnamization," and "Peace with Honor," among others, are examples of the iconography that confused a generation of Americans. Consider the circumstances of the "protective reaction" offensive that began the wider air war in 1964.

The U.S. Navy destroyers *Maddox* and *C. Turner Joy* were attacked while on patrol during the night of August 4, 1964, in the Gulf of Tonkin. Hours after this attack by North Vietnamese gunboats, President Lyndon Johnson ordered the first bombing raids against North Vietnam. Within one week, Congress had passed the Gulf of Tonkin resolution authorizing the President of the United States to "take all the necessary steps" to "prevent further aggression" in Vietnam.

Here is how *Time* described the Gulf of Tonkin attack:

The night glowed eerily with the nightmarish glare of air-dropped flares and boats' searchlights. For three and a half hours the small boats attacked in pass after pass. Ten enemy torpedoes sizzled through the water. Each time the skippers, tracking the fish by radar, maneuvered to evade them. Gunfire and gun smells and shouts stung the air. Two of the enemy boats went down. Then, at 1:30 a.m., the remaining PTs ended the fight, roared off through the black night to the north.

And in *Newsweek:*

The U.S. ships blazed out salvo after salvo of shells. Torpedoes whipped by, some only 100 feet from the destroyers' beams. A PT boat burst into flames and sank. More U.S. jets swooped in. . . . Another PT boat exploded and sank, and then the others scurried off into the darkness nursing their wounds. The battle was won. Now it was time for American might to strike back.[6]

The iconography of Tonkin fitted the "color" writer's vision of the quintessential naval battle. Only much later, thanks to Senator William Fulbright, Senator Wayne

Morse, the Foreign Relations Committee staff, the correspondent Joseph Goulden, and a small group of other senators and journalists, did the real story of the engagement emerge. The two destroyers actually were on an intelligence-gathering mission within 12 miles of the North Vietnamese coastline; the destroyers had turned on their gun control equipment in order to "light up" the North Vietnamese defense electronics—that is, trigger the other side to turn on their shore radars so that the locations could be plotted electronically. Because of the cloud-shrouded, poor night visibility and an electrical storm, no seaman actually saw any "attacking" North Vietnamese patrol boats. When the confusion and shouting stopped aboard the American destroyers, crew members were questioned, and a cable was sent to higher headquarters:

Review of action makes many reported contacts and torpedoes fired appear doubtful. . . .Freak weather effects and overeager sonarmen may have accounted for many reports. No actual visual sightings by *Maddox*. Suggest complete evaluation before any further action.

The signal never made it back in time to the White House (or to the news media).

Eight years and over a million casualties—American and Vietnamese—later, U.S. ground troops left Vietnam under the cover of a new iconography. The term was "Vietnamization," which was intended to mean the gradual takeover of the American war effort by the troops of the Saigon government. Vietnamization became the "story." In March 1969, Av Westin, the executive producer of the "ABC Evening News," sent a Telex to the ABC News Saigon bureau. It read, in part:

I think the time has come to shift some of our focus from the battlefield, or more specifically American military involvement with the enemy, to themes and stories under the general heading: We Are On Our Way Out Of Vietnam. . . .[7]

The Nixon Administration strategy of Vietnamization dictated the invasion of Cambodia to destroy the enemy's "sanctuary" and its "Supreme" headquarters or, as it was called in stories, the "jungle Pentagon" (more iconography). On May 2, 1970, two days after President Nixon sent U.S. combat troops into Cambodia, the United Press International lead story from Saigon read:

Allied troops and tanks resumed their advance into neighboring Cambodia early today, one American tank column pressing to within 6,000 yards of an underground tunnel complex thought to be the site of the Communist military command headquarters for the war in Vietnam.

It was, as James McCartney of the Knight Newspapers later wrote, war in all its drama: a tank column slashing toward an objective, the enemy headquarters about to fall. It was the beginning of a month of such set-piece copy about the new war in Cambodia. But, writes McCartney, if the consumer had paid close attention to the news bulletins in the days to follow, he would find out that

the U.S. tank column was riding into monsoon mud and rain, and the Communist military command headquarters was evanescent and elusive, nowhere to be found. . . . For somehow, despite all the tank columns, the allied "thrusts," the "new assaults," the fire bases, when ground action by U.S. troops was finished two months later the Communists had gobbled up almost half of Cambodia. By October they controlled more than half of it.

"With all that action," McCartney asks, "how did the Communists quietly take over so much terrain?" And he answers,

What happened was what has almost always happened in Vietnam when U.S. power has been used in grand, military "sweeps." What happened was that guerrillas, in a guerrilla war, acted like guerrillas. They faded into the jungle or the countryside or villages. They fell back and spread out and disappeared, letting the U.S. and the South Vietnamese destroy thousands of acres of jungle and countryside and caches of supplies while they bided their time, as guerrillas will.

"The casual reader of U.S. newspapers, the TV viewer, or the listener to radio bulletins," McCartney concludes, "would find that hard to discern, for it was not the war he had read or heard about or seen on the tube."[8]

The incursion into Laos, a year later, produced a similar iconography—and somewhat similar results. Again, bold spearheads were thrusting toward the heavy black line on newspaper and television maps labeled *Ho Chi Minh Trail.* The image of a well-marked, definite, physical entity presented itself. But the deeper into Laos the Saigon forces went, the vaguer the nightly news reports got. Instead of writing or speaking about the *Ho Chi Minh Trail,* the reports began to adopt another usage: it was now the *Ho Chi Minh Trail network.* A few miles deeper into Laos and this entity became the *complex system of paths that make up the Ho Chi Minh Trail network.* As the Saigon troops went deeper into Laos, the truth gradually emerged: perhaps all of Southern Laos was the *Ho Chi Minh Trail.* Or, as Gloria Emerson later observed, "The Ho Chi Minh Trail was a state of mind."

So much iconography has been fabricated by the officials of four American administrations that it is hard to see how the media could have been taken in so consistently. Yet, on October 26, 1972, there was the spectacle of Henry Kissinger declaring on national television that "Peace is at hand." And the next week there was a dove fluttering on the cover of *Time* magazine and on the *Newsweek* cover a GI helmet with the words "Goodbye, Vietnam" stenciled on it. Peace wasn't at hand. Three months later, in January 1973, something called "Peace with Honor" was at hand, and American soldiers were being photographed and filmed for the story of the "Last Troops Leaving Vietnam."

Winding Down the Coverage

The bombing of Cambodia continued through March 1973; and some 100,000 American servicemen remained in the Indochina military theater, many stationed aboard U.S. Navy vessels. About 50,000 were U.S. Air Force officers and men based in Thailand. In addition to the 100,000 men in uniform, another 10,000 remained in Vietnam as "advisers" working for the Saigon government and for civilian U.S. agencies. But while the U.S. presence in Indochina continued, information about that presence was reduced. The daily news briefings in Saigon ended on January 28, 1973, when the cease-fire agreement went into effect. The U.S. Military Assistance Command Information Office in Saigon went out of business on March 29, 1973, the deadline for the withdrawal of American troops from Vietnam. One of the MACOI officers said, "It's up to us to switch off the light at the end of the tunnel." His joke made an unintended point; the press was in the dark once again. Or, more properly, its attention had gone on to other "news," once American lives were no longer being lost. The size of American news bureaus in Saigon shrank, and in some cases were taken over by non-Americans or closed down completely. The Indochina coverage had come full circle—to return to a stage of benign neglect again. The "peace" achieved in Vietnam by the 1973 cease-fire agreement repeated the pattern of the *less visible*—to Western eyes—Indochina conflicts of 1954 through 1961. The final bitter tragedy of the 12-year-long American intervention in Indochina was that government and press—the one consciously, the other unthinkingly—had succeeded in winding down the coverage of the war, rather than the war itself.

When, in the spring of 1975, the inevitable occurred and the Saigon forces crumbled quickly under the final Northern offensive, it was still possible for large numbers of the American news audience to be surprised by the outcome. How was it, many people wondered, that the North was able to defeat the South? Was it the fault of the U.S. Congress? Or perhaps the Chinese and Russian arms made the difference? Or was it that Saigon had bad leadership? The nature and direction of the "enemy" remained "elusive" and "enigmatic" until the end.

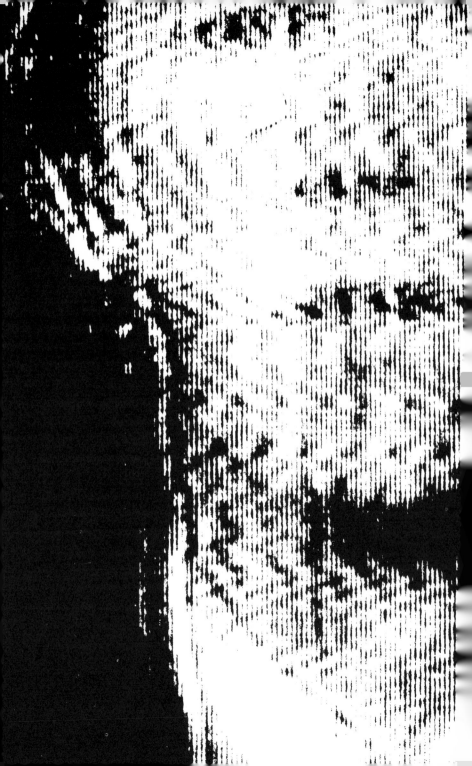

Chapter 7
Pentagon Papers:
The "Secret History" of Ellsberg[1]

When Daniel Ellsberg turned himself in to the United States Attorney's Office in Boston in connection with the Pentagon Papers case, he freely admitted that he was the former government analyst who had made the "secret history" of the Vietnam War available to the *New York Times*. "I did this clearly in my own jeopardy," he declared, "and I am prepared to answer all the consequences of these decisions. That includes the personal consequences to me and my family, whatever these may be. Would you not go to prison to help end this war?" The date was June 28, 1971.

A week or two later, however, the Gallup poll reported that about half the American public did not have any idea what the Pentagon Papers were—much less how they might help end the Vietnam War—almost a month after their publication by the *Times*. The release of the Pentagon Papers and the government's attempt to stop their publication had commanded the largest headlines and the top of the television news programs for almost a month. Why, then, the wide public ignorance? One clue lies in the press's initial inattentiveness. During the first days after the *Times* ran its initial disclosures on June 13, the press's response to the documents was underwhelming.

On the Saturday night and Sunday morning when the first story appeared, *New York Times* editors grouped around the wire service tickers and their television sets straining for some sign that someone had looked at the 10,000-plus words written by reporter Neil Sheehan and at the accompanying three pages of government memoranda; it turned out to be a long and uneventful day. However, when the focus of events shifted—as a result of the stupefying overreaction of the Nixon Administration—from the actual content of the Papers to the right of the papers to publish them—the press's response was electric: a "historic battle" had been joined between Government and Press. The First Amendment was at stake. In all the drama of unfolding conflict, the Papers, which were a dry political narrative of the American involvement in Vietnam, were lost, and never wholly found again.

An Unimpressive Start

While the readers of the *Times* had their first look at the Pentagon Papers story on Sunday morning, all of the national news organizations had, theoretically, an earlier start. About 5:00 P.M., Saturday, June 12, the *New York Times* News Service, which has some 300 subscribers, put a note on the leased wire connecting its offices to the offices of its clients saying that at 6:00 P.M. it would begin to transmit a major exclusive story. In addition, the News Service phoned about ten of its "best" newspaper clients to give them more details. Despite this alert, the initial installment received generally spotty treatment among *Times* subscribers. The *Louisville Courier-Journal* featured the story prominently; the *Portland Oregonian* and the *Chicago Tribune* were more typical, passing up the first installment—and the second and third—for an entire week. Pickups by *Times* subscribers overseas, according to Rob Roy Buckingham of the *Times* News Service, "was not very impressive either."

The Associated Press is the largest news organization in the United States; it is a cooperative and is entitled to use stories originated by members like the *Times*. On major news breaks, there is usually an "embargo" for one cycle; that is, the AP won't put a member's "exclusive" on the wire until after noon or after midnight, whichever comes first. With major stories, however, embargoes are usually ignored. In the case of the Pentagon Papers, the AP editors didn't even ask to break the embargo. The AP sent nothing on its wires Saturday night or all day Sunday or Sunday night; not until Monday afternoon did the AP carry a story. Equally remarkable, there were no callbacks or complaints from any of the AP's 4,500 newspaper and radio-television station members. "When you have a major development," says an AP executive, "you usually expect immediate rockets from the members. . . ."

At the United Press International, the first story on the Pentagon Papers wasn't sent until Sunday afternoon. According to Roger Tatarian, at the time UPI general manager, the story was "several hundred" words long, though it was not designated a "budget item"–one of the major stories called to the attention of subscribers. Tatarian, who says he was "safely out of the country" that weekend, thinks his editors should have carried the story earlier. Editors of *Time* and *Newsweek* also received the Sunday *Times*'s first edition in the office about 9:00 P.M. that Saturday night, but neither magazine bothered to remake a page in order to take note of the *Times*'s revelations. In 1971, both *Time* and *Newsweek* were on a schedule calling for transmission of all copy to their midwestern printing plants by Saturday night; press runs began late Sunday morning. Although the newsmagazines normally try to get in material that will keep their products looking "fresh" the seven days they are on the newsstands, both *Time* and *Newsweek* were under economic

'S-MAKING "SYSTEM" . . . WHODL

pressures to hold costs down and close on time. "At 10 p.m. that Saturday," recalls *Time* Senior Editor Jason McManus, "we read the *Times* story and made the decision not to do a twenty-minute re-write. In this case we stepped back and did things thoroughly the next week." Managing Editor Henry A. Grunwald was out of the country at the time; a few months earlier, in one of his periodic tours of the provincial bureaus, a "foreign policy night" was arranged in Cambridge with Harvard and MIT faculty; after dinner, an intense guest named Daniel Ellsberg lectured Grunwald—"quite vehemently"—on Vietnam. Ellsberg also pressed into Grunwald's hands a long manuscript on the Vietnam War he was trying, unsuccessfully, to get published.

The newsroom at ABC News in New York also gets its copies of the *Times* on Saturday night. Although there is no late Saturday night ABC News program, ABC's "Issues and Answers" program that Sunday featured Senator Hubert Humphrey as its guest. Not a word was mentioned about the Papers. "It was a very sad day for us," recalls William Sheehan, at the time director of television news at ABC. "We really didn't pick up the story until Monday. When I asked Bill Beutel [on the 11:00 P.M. Sunday news] and the reporters on 'Issues and Answers' what happened, I was told, 'The *Times* story looked like one of those things that would be important, so we put it aside to read. . . .' " Sheehan, who read his *Times* while on a Sunday morning plane to California, acknowledged that "it is one of those things you need plenty of time to read. . . ."

Defense Secretary Melvin Laird was due on the CBS News "Face the Nation" program that Sunday. Laird was so sure he would be asked embarrassing questions about

NIT? . . . CBS, NBC, AND ABC DECL

what the Pentagon planned to do about the *Times*'s publication of the study that he and Attorney General John Mitchell had worked out an answer of sorts (its thrust was that the government was looking into the matter). In the warm-up period before air time, CBS News Correspondent George Herman chatted with Laird about the *Times* story. But neither Herman nor the other correspondents bothered to ask Laird anything on camera.

That night, on the "CBS Sunday News with Dan Rather," Correspondent Rather took note of the *second* article in the *Times* series, in its Monday, June 14, editions. The CBS item ran thirty seconds:

RATHER: *The New York Times* reports tonight that, according to a secret Pentagon study, the Johnson Administration reached a general consensus to bomb North Vietnam as early as September, 1964, five months before the order to begin air attacks on the North actually went into effect.
   The *Times* story points out that the consensus on bombing came at the height of the Presidential campaign during which Johnson's opponent, Senator Barry Goldwater, advocated full-scale bombing of North Vietnam.

Monday morning, the "CBS Morning News with John Hart" clustered the Pentagon Papers with a miscellany of other "military" items:

HART: A big Air Force transport plane is missing in the Pacific with 24 men on it. The C-135 was flying from American Samoa to Hawaii.
   American headquarters in Saigon says B-52's unloaded 500 tons of bombs on the jungle below the demilitarized zone, because they figure that a lot of Communist troops are massing there . . . the intelligence people thinking that they want to make an attack to influence the October elections. Bernie.

.. HUMAN INTEREST, PRESS INTE

KALB: *The Washington Post* reports this morning that the White House has no copy of that highly secret governmental study of US involvement in Vietnam. The first installment of that study was published in yesterday's *New York Times.* And in its latest installment, published in *The Times* this morning, the newspaper reports that a consensus to bomb North Vietnam developed before the 1964 presidential election.

The secret Pentagon study of the Vietnam war, as reported by *The Times,* states that the Johnson Administration reached that general consensus at a White House strategy meeting on September 7th, 1964. That is that air attacks against the North would probably have to be launched. *The Times* notes that the administration consensus came at the height of the presidential election contest between President Johnson and Senator Goldwater, whose advocacy of full-scale air attacks against the North had become a major issue. The last round of detailed planning of various political and military strategies for a bombing campaign began in earnest, the study says, on November 3rd, 1964—the day that Lyndon Johnson was elected President in his own right.

The Times report came as both houses of Congress were getting ready for a vote this week, probably Wednesday, on legislating all US forces out. . . .

NBC alone among the major news organizations appeared to have its wits about it that weekend. "I read *The Times* on Sunday morning," says Wallace Westfield, then the executive producer of the "NBC Nightly News," at that time, "and said to myself, 'my God, what a story they have here.' . . ." David Brinkley, at the NBC News Washington studio, and Washington producer Dave Tietlebaum were also impressed. Tietlebaum made the Pentagon Papers story the lead item on the Sunday evening network program, devoting almost 10 minutes of the 22 editorial minutes to the story. Anchorman Brinkley said:

RESTS . . . EPILOGUE: THE PLUMB

Good evening . . .

Four years ago . . . Defense Secretary Robert McNamara
was deeply disillusioned with the Vietnam war . . . then
raging at full blast . . . and he ordered a detailed study of
just how the United States got into it.

The study occupied about 40 people for more than a
year . . . and it was first made public today . . . in *The
New York Times.*

It says the first mistake was when the Truman Administration gave assistance to the French, then fighting a colonial war trying to hold on to its colony, Vietnam.

The Eisenhower and Kennedy Administrations expanded
the American commitment . . . and then the Johnson
Administration made it into a full-scale war, in the open.

It says Johnson had secret plans to make it a real war . . .
waited for a public excuse . . . and whatever happened in
the Gulf of Tonkin . . . if anything happened . . . brought
the excuse. And the war was on.

The CIA is said to have been right all along, urging the
U.S. to stay out . . . but was not listened to. It said the
Air Force plan for bombing would do no good.

So . . . the report seems to show the U.S. got into a war
. . . in the beginning . . . by trying to help other countries
fight theirs . . . and going on and on from there.

The program then shifted to correspondent Paul Duke,
who interviewed Senator Stuart Symington.

The News-Making "System"
Why didn't the *Times* story attract more immediate attention? The answers hint at how news judgments, and mis-
judgments, are really made. An AP editor said, "Sure, it
was a magnificent job in some ways, but to tell you the
truth I wasn't that impressed at first. A lot of it sounded
familiar, and there was a certain tendentious quality to

CONNECTION

Neil Sheehan's piece. . . . Of course, they had those documents, but when you think of trying to boil it all down to wire service size, it's tough." UPI's Roger Tatarian thought that the *Times*'s understated style put everyone off; the *Times* headlined the story VIETNAM ARCHIVE: PENTAGON STUDY TRACES 3 DECADES OF GROWING U.S. INVOLVEMENT. "In the absence of a label," Tatarian said, "the thing just sneaks up on you. You read the first few paragraphs and you think, 'aw shucks, not much here. . . .'" A CBS executive allowed that "the Sunday *Times* sometimes puts us to sleep." McManus of *Time* said that "the documents required time to step back and analyze; what was new, what wasn't new. . . ." Peter Goldman of *Newsweek* added, "There was that gray aura of history about it; the stuff didn't get vivid until it got into Lyndon Johnson the second and third day." ABC's Sheehan offered this opinion: "I've spent hours thinking about why the story wasn't covered better. There was the low-key approach and the voluminousness of the documents. But I don't think there was any attempt to hold back or to play the government's game."

Outsiders and critics of the press tend to see other reasons, of course. It is hard for them to understand that the press usually acts the way it does out of plain bad habits rather than for important political reasons. In the case of the Pentagon Papers, the initial inattention was more a matter of low energy levels, "cost consciousness," poor news judgments, the normal professional disinterest in "dry" histories and "gray" documents—as well as who was on vacation and all the other nonobjective influences on the news—rather than any highly politicized decision making. Even the *Times*'s decision to publish was shaped by these nonobjective factors.[2] The *Times* received the documents from Ellsberg sometime before the end of March 1971; eventually some 75 news and production people were working on the writing and editing of the mass of documents—the full history ran to 2.5 million words in 47 volumes—in order to accomplish the task in "the *Times'* way"—that is, with an attention to detail and a completeness that can't be matched by any other news organization in the world. But, as Sanford Ungar reports in his excellent study, *The Papers and the Papers,*

This arduous and agonizing process might have gone on for several weeks more had not *Times* publisher Arthur Ochs Sulzberger made plans to fly to London for a board meeting on the weekend of June 13 and then to vacation in Europe with his family; the publisher had set that weekend as a deadline for major decisions concerning the Papers. Sulzberger gave the final go-ahead only in a last-minute meeting in his office on Friday morning June 11.[3]

The go-ahead was given with the third installment still in Neil Sheehan's typewriter.

Whodunit?

The *Times*—and the country—can thank the Nixon Administration for stirring up interest in a flagging story. Late in the afternoon of Monday, June 14, the AP sent an "urgent" message out of Washington saying that the *Times* had been notified that the Justice Department was seeking to stop publication. Still later, the word was leaked at the Pentagon that a former government official named Daniel Ellsberg was being sought by the FBI as the suspected leak. At this point, the Pentagon Papers struck the knee-jerk reflexes of the media. It became a First

Amendment contest as well as a cops-and-robbers story: Whodunit? Now the silent wires began to hum. "If the government had cooled it," claims an AP editor, "the story would have been cut in half and then died. . . ."

The Pentagon Papers narrative effectively ended in 1968 before the Nixon Administration took office. The documents depicted both Republican and Democratic presidents in a harsh light: the Truman Administration "directly involved" the United States in Indochina through aid to the Colonial French; the Eisenhower Administration undermined the Geneva settlement of 1954; John F. Kennedy expanded the American involvement into a "broad commitment"; finally, Lyndon Johnson followed a "provocative strategy" and widened the war while deceiving the Congress and the public. The material concerning Johnson was the most devastating politically.

According to Sanford Ungar, Senator Robert Dole, at the time the chairman of the Republican National Committee, argued against going to court and urged the Republicans to exploit the Papers for what they revealed about their Democratic predecessors. Instead of following Dole's advice, the Administration decided on a hard-line law-and-order approach against this "massive security breach."

Two major figures in the Watergate break-in and cover-up conspiracy—Attorney General John Mitchell and Robert Mardian, the head of the Justice Department's Internal Security Division—sent the *Times* an urgent telegram invoking the provisions of the Espionage Law about publishing "information relating to the national defense." The *Times* declined to cease publication of the third installment of the Papers; but the "play" on the front page of

the *Times* the next morning reflected the shift away from
the Vietnam history to the Government-Press confrontation. The *Times*'s lead article was MITCHELL SEEKS TO
HALT SERIES ON VIETNAM BUT TIMES REFUSES.
"Think what it would have meant in our history and in
the history of the newspaper business," A. M. "Abe"
Rosenthal, the *Times*'s managing editor, noted some
months later, "if the headline had been 'Justice Department Asks End to Vietnam Series and Times Concedes.'
I think it would have changed the history of the newspaper business."[4] But Sanford Ungar believes that the
decision to play the story about the confrontation over
the Pentagon Papers so prominently may also have shifted
the focus of attention away from further interest in the
Vietnam history. "Never mind what the Papers said; were
the papers entitled to publish articles based on them?"

CBS, NBC, and ABC Decline

The next day the government obtained a temporary restraining order enjoining the *Times* from publishing any
more of the Papers—the first time in the nation's history
that a newspaper was restrained in advance by a court
from publishing a specific article. Ellsberg and a small
group of associates, concerned that their efforts to get the
story out were "losing momentum," decided to go elsewhere. The *Washington Post,* the *Boston Globe,* the *Chicago Sun-Times,* the *St. Louis Post-Dispatch,* the *Los
Angeles Times,* the *Christian Science Monitor,* among
other newspapers, blossomed forth with Vietnam Archive
documents—as if a Johnny Appleseed had been at work
across the land. Ellsberg's efforts had more equivocal results at the networks. If they had been slow to grasp the

meaning of the first stories, now they seemed cautious about their own involvement.

According to *Washington Post* reporter Robert J. Samuelson, at least two of the major television networks were offered the Pentagon Papers, but both decided not to use the documents.[5] CBS News President Richard Salant told Samuelson that CBS was offered portions of the papers on June 17, two days after the temporary restraining order against the *Times* was granted. The material, Salant said, was offered "on an immediate release basis from sources who were in a terrible rush to get these things published." CBS declined, he said, because it wanted to study the documents "and put them in journalistic context." However, the offer of the documents did lead to an exclusive Walter Cronkite interview with Daniel Ellsberg.

Bill Sheehan of ABC News told Samuelson that on June 23 or 24 his network was offered "1,000 pages of fresh papers." Before the Papers would be delivered, Sheehan said, ABC would have had to agree that it would not let existing injunctions against newspapers inhibit it from using the Papers. ABC declined to do so. The network's attorneys raised the prospect of citations for contempt of court.

According to another inquiring reporter, Steve Knoll, who worked for *Variety* at the time of the Pentagon Papers case, substantial portions of the study were offered to NBC on Sunday, June 20, in a telephone call. A spokesman for NBC President Julian Goodman later told Knoll, "We were offered the Pentagon Papers on a severely proscribed basis. We asked for an opportunity to do an orderly journalistic job; they wanted a hasty presentation of a huge volume of material. We told them that on that

basis we had no interest." Six months later at a meeting
of the International Radio and Television Society, NBC's
John Chancellor commented, "I wonder what *The New
York Times* would have done . . . if somebody had offered
them 50,000 feet of 16 millimeter film. The analogy is
exact in our terms. There are some things that we can't
carry."

While declining the June 20 phone offer, NBC did ex-
press an interest in putting Ellsberg on the air, according
to Knoll. The caller—either Ellsberg or an associate—said
he would think it over. Then on Wednesday, June 23,
Ellsberg appeared on CBS News with Walter Cronkite.
According to Knoll, Ellsberg offered to come on NBC
after that, but NBC declined to follow CBS since, as an
NBC News official told the reporter, "Ellsberg had answered almost all the questions we would have asked" in
his conversation with Cronkite.

Chancellor told the International Radio and Television
Society forum, "Dan Ellsberg called me up about this
time. We'd been trying, along with Walter [Cronkite] and
Harry [Reasoner], quite desperately for three or four days
to find him . . . and so one night—it troubled my indiges-
tion—I saw Walter on the box with Dan Ellsberg. About
three days later, my thirty or forty telephone messages
were answered by Ellsberg or actually his lawyer, and
they said, 'You can have him now, he's very anxious to
appear on your program' . . . and we just said the hell
with it." NBC had been "scooped," and in the network
news business's way of looking at the world, Ellsberg and
the Pentagon Papers were no longer "newsworthy" enough
for a Chancellor interview. The "normal" coverage would
be sufficient.

Television's sole original contribution, then, was the CBS interview with Ellsberg, who was still underground (he merely checked into the Fenway Motor Inn on Memorial Drive in Cambridge). Gordon Manning, an aggressive and talented veteran newsman, and a CBS vice-president at the time, arranged the coup. When Cronkite, Manning, and Ellsberg met, according to Knoll, Ellsberg produced a two-foot-high stack of Pentagon Papers. He wanted them reported on the air. Manning wanted to put together a special report, using clips from the Ellsberg interview as well as film of Walt W. Rostow, Henry Cabot Lodge, and other principals. The idea went "Upstairs," and CBS decided against it. "Ellsberg wanted it done immediately," Manning later said. "I needed time for film and tape research. He had a timetable of getting out as much material as fast as possible. [Moreover] the *Times* had already printed the best stuff."

Human Interest, Press Interests
Cronkite, in his interview, concentrated on drawing out "Ellsberg the man" and his "motivations"—the "human interest" approach to the news. Ellsberg at one point said, "All the questions so far have been based, I think, on a slightly wrong premise, and that is that the heart of the study is out. . . . That's far from true. . . . There's a lot more to come. . . ." In the days and weeks that followed, the "heart of the study" receded further and further from view. The details of America's lurching march in the quagmire of Vietnam were at once enormously painful and instructive. But they could not compete with the current news, the Freedom of the Press fight. The *Washington Post* was also restrained from publishing the Papers—and

then the *Boston Globe* and the *St. Louis Post-Dispatch.* The Washington and New York cases moved quickly through the Courts of Appeals and to the United States Supreme Court, which delivered a dramatic 6 to 3 decision affirming the newspapers' right to publish. There were nine separate opinion essays. Among the majority, Justice Hugo Black delivered the "absolutist" position: "I believe that every moment's continuance of the injunctions against these newspapers amounts to a flagrant, indefensible and continuing violation of the First Amendment. . . ." U.S. Attorney Whitney North Seymour, in his brief to the Court of Appeals in the *Times* case, had argued that the only issues were "whether a newspaper in possession of stolen Top Secret documents vital to the national defense is free to publish them in its sole discretion" and "whether newspaper publication of military intelligence secrets may be enjoined for the purpose of protecting national security." Justice Harry Blackmun, in his dissenting opinion, picked up this theme; Blackmun spoke worriedly of the "harm"—"the death of soldiers, the destruction of alliances"—that might be done to the nation by publication.

Epilogue: The Plumbers' Connection

An unintended rebuttal to the government argument was supplied three years later—by Richard Nixon himself. The Nixon decision to tape-record his own private conversations provided evidence that the blanket of "national security" was a thin and tacky construction at best. On July 24, 1971, less than a month after the Supreme Court decision permitted newspapers to resume publication of the Pentagon Papers, Nixon met with John Ehrlichman and with Egil Krogh, the young aide in charge of the "plumbers" unit created by the White House to look into leaks and perform other odd jobs. The day before the *New York Times* had carried an account of the prospective U.S. negotiating position in the strategic arms limitation talks (SALT) with the Soviet Union. The transcript of the conversation, prepared by the House Judiciary Committee staff as part of its impeachment proceedings, shows the President furious at a Pentagon employee believed to be the source of the news leak. Move in on him, "polygraph" him, the President demands. Then:

P   Well, I just think we ought to go out ahead and it, it does happen. This does affect the national security—this particular one. This isn't like the Pentagon Papers. This one involves a current negotiation and it should not have been, and it, its getting out jeopardizes the negotiating position. Now, God damn it, we're not going to allow it. We just aren't going to allow it.

E or K   All right.

P   Good luck.

The President had already put the Pentagon Papers "security" case behind him. It was still, of course, a political issue for Charles Colson, the premier White House hatchet man. According to White House documents released by the House Judiciary Committee in July 1974, Colson spent a great deal of his time thinking how he could use Daniel Ellsberg—"a natural villain," Colson called him—"to arouse the heartland which at present is not very excited about the whole [Pentagon Papers] issue."

"To arouse the heartland" had been one of Ellsberg's goals as well when he put the whole train of events in motion. One measure of how well he succeeded is contained in the Gallup poll that registered widespread ignorance of the Papers. The *Times* resumed its series and eventually published ten installments. A Bantam Books paperback edition of the *Times* material sold over a million copies at $2.25 a copy; a Beacon Press hard-cover edition sold about 2,000 copies (out of 20,000 printed); 500 copies of a U.S. Government Printing Office version were sold. One evening late in 1971, Daniel Ellsberg appeared before a standing-room-only crowd of 1,200 young men and women at the Kresge auditorium on the MIT campus in Cambridge. It was clearly an admiring audience. The students gave him their close attention for well over two hours. But when he asked for a show of hands of all those who had read the Pentagon Papers, no more than one or two hands went up. Ellsberg was not surprised. I wasn't either.

Chapter 8
"I'll Never Forget What's His Name?"

Al Smith once observed that "America is a ten day country." In the mid-1960s, a number of black ghettos in major cities erupted into violence and rioting. A commission headed by former Governor Otto Kerner of Illinois was established to study the roots of the civil disorders and, in due time, issued its report.[1] One of the widely quoted sections of the report said that the failure of the news media to provide day-to-day coverage of the black and Puerto Rican communities had created an atmosphere of misunderstanding and mistrust that was contributing to the black-white schism in the country. "The news media," the Kerner Commission Report said, "have not communicated to the majority of their audience—which is white—a sense of the degradation, misery, and hopelessness of living in the ghetto. They have not communicated to whites a feeling for the difficulties and frustrations of being a Negro in the United States. They have not shown understanding or appreciation of—and thus have not communicated—a sense of Negro culture, thought, or history."

There followed a great deal of hand-wringing, soul-searching, and solemn talk by publishers and broadcasters about the responsibility to hire more blacks and minority group members in the newsroom and to devote more time and space in news columns and news broadcasts to minority matters. But then urban violence changed from large-scale riots to smaller, seemingly aberrant "incidents." And as the long hot summers cooled, it wasn't long before many publishers and broadcasters forgot their brave resolutions.

The content of programming and news on television is one measure of minority "progress" in the years since the Kerner Commission Report. Television is often pictured as the primary "racial medium" in the United States. Poor people watch more television than middle-class people, and the non-white poor watch more television than the white poor. "Black" and "brown" sets are on as much as seven hours per day per family. (See pp. 152–153.) Tony Brown, executive producer of "Black Journal," once a fixture on public television, observed at a meeting in Washington a few years ago that "we see more white doves fly in the kitchen, more white women thinking about their whiter than white wash, more white teeth with sex appeal, more white June brides and more coloreds acting white." Black people also tend to get more of their news and information from broadcasting than from print sources (newspaper reading is not a ghetto habit). According to the Louis Harris polls, black people tend to trust television news more than they do newspapers.

"Progress" since 1968

Two years after the Kerner Report, Jean Fairfax of the NAACP Legal Defense Fund told a meeting of representatives of the broadcasting industry that their programming "presents a daily reminder of the unwillingness of white America to deal with black Americans as mature, serious, complex human beings."[2] One Sunday in the spring of 1970, Ms. Fairfax said she spent 11 hours watching a major television station in Philadelphia, where she lives. "During 10 hours, 29 minutes and 45 seconds of broadcasting time, the only black face I saw was a seal! No blacks interpreted current issues. No blacks were

'PROGRESS" SINCE 1968 . . . SOU▶

solicited for their opinions in the interviews. No blacks participated in the dramas or the quiz shows. No blacks were on the commercials. Black Americans were invisible."

Later that year, a study prepared for the Legal Defense Fund confirmed Ms. Fairfax's impressions.[3] The study monitored the frequency and nature of black appearances on television commercials carried during sports broadcasts; the cities studied were New York, Memphis, Charlotte, and Birmingham, all cities with large black populations. Since so many black athletes participate in such events as football, basketball, and baseball—they are, in a very real way, the field hands for big-time sports broadcasting—it seemed reasonable to expect to see some black faces in the commercials. The study found that "in all four cities, most of the Negro commercial appearance was limited to momentary flashes."

Four years later, in 1974, there had not been much change: a few more black faces in flashes on a few more commercials; a few more black discussion programs on local stations ("Ebony Beat" in Atlanta, "Say Brother" in Boston); and on the networks, a few more black situation comedies with blacks acting like blacks ("Sanford and Son") rather than like whites ("Julia"). The networks invariably schedule the "serious" black programs on Saturdays and Sundays—giving a pointed meaning to television's weekend ghetto of public service broadcasting. Black-oriented efforts such as CBS's "Black Arts" ran on Sunday mornings and NBC's "Positively Black" on Sunday afternoons. This programming pattern, at least, is color-blind: NBC put "Positively Black" opposite the highly rated Sunday professional sports just as it used to

LEVERAGE . . .CABLE FABLES . .

Television Viewing: Black and White Choices

Chicago		Detroit		Washington	
Black	Total Metro	Black	Total Metro	Black	Total Metro

Chicago: Black 51 hr, 40 min; Total Metro 42 hr, 50 min

Detroit: Black 54 hr, 11 min; Total Metro 45 hr, 22 min

Washington: Black 47 hr, 53 min; Total Metro 39 hr, 41 min

Black households watch television "significantly" more than households generally, the A. C. Nielsen Company found in special studies in the metropolitan areas of five major markets. Just how much more is shown in the city-by-city graphs above (which describe black versus total metropolitan TV household viewing in terms of average hours per week for the 7:00 A.M. to 1:00 A.M. broadcast day).

In three markets for which day-part detail was available—Chicago, Detroit, and Washington—Nielsen said higher levels of black usage were evident in almost all day-parts but most pronounced in Monday–Friday daytime and early fringe. Prime time accounted for the largest blocks of viewing among both black households and total households but represented a lower percentage of total viewing among blacks than among households generally.

. THE USE OF PRESSURE . . . COLC

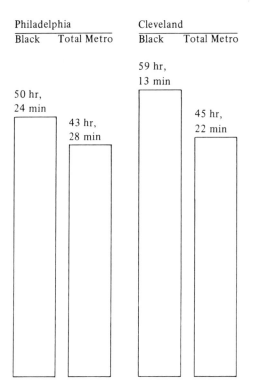

Philadelphia		Cleveland	
Black	Total Metro	Black	Total Metro
50 hr, 24 min	43 hr, 28 min	59 hr, 13 min	45 hr, 22 min

Not surprisingly, the study also found that programs featuring blacks tend to get higher ratings in black households than in total households. On a total-households basis, "Sanford and Son," for instance, ranked first in Detroit, second in Washington, and third in Chicago, although in none of those markets with more than a 41 rating, while on a black-households basis it ranked first in all three markets with 69 ratings in Chicago and Washington and a 74 in Detroit. "Soul Train" didn't make the top ten in any of the three cities but ranked second in black households in Detroit and Washington and, though eighth in Chicago, was credited with helping to lift black-household set usage there to a Saturday daytime peak at its 2:00 P.M. air time.

Source: Courtesy of *Broadcasting*, October 14, 1974.

ND? . . . THE GARY CONVENTION

put its news specials against ABC's enormously popular "Marcus Welby, M.D." on Tuesday nights; that way, as a network man once explained, the logbook shows time for public affairs programs while the rating book concedes a time strip the opposition would dominate in any case.

Local programming "aimed" at blacks increased in those cities where the black population has been increasing. A minor but significant "breakthrough" occurred when blacks and other minority groups began losing their unenviable status as the "invisible audience" of television. Les Brown, television reporter for the *New York Times,* reported in his book, *Television: The Business Behind the Box,* that the Nielsen Company and other surveyors of the American television audience didn't start putting their recorders in black homes until 1971 and 1972; the advertisers, it seems, were not interested in the program preferences of black consumers until they were confronted with the facts of the increasing buying power of minority groups.

Soul and Leverage

Tokenism is the usual description of these practices, but there isn't even a token in the upper proprietary levels of broadcasting. Of the 863 commercial television stations in the United States, not one was owned or operated by a racial minority group member, as of September 1974. Not even black-oriented "soul" radio is firmly in the hands of blacks. According to the Race Relations Information Center of Nashville, Tennessee, about 9 of the estimated 350 "soul" stations in the United States were owned by blacks. At last count, none of the 202 public television stations in the continental United States had a

. . . THE SPOOK BY THE DOOR

black station manager, although there was a black executive at the public television station in the U.S. Virgin Islands. A few black people do sit in executive or policy-making positions in the broadcasting industry; Franklin A. Thomas, president of the Bedford Stuyvesant Restoration Corporation, joined the board of directors of CBS in 1971, and Benjamin Hooks was named to the Federal Communications Commission in the spring of 1972, the first black commissioner in the history of the FCC.[4] But generally, from the white writers of the successful "black" comedy "Sanford and Son" on NBC to the white executives who prescreened public television's "Black Journal," it is obvious that blacks do not exert real leverage in broadcasting. Blacks may have some high-sounding titles; but as Matthew Robinson of the Children's Television Workshop (producers of "Sesame Street") told the Black Congressional Caucus meeting in 1972, "I don't know of a program for which a black man can determine if it remains on the air, how it remains on the air and how it gets on the air in the first place."

On several occasions, black businessmen, political leaders, and educators have explored the possibilities of minority ownership of broadcasting properties. A group meeting at Howard University which included New York *Amsterdam News* publisher Clarence Jones a few years ago seriously discussed the purchase of the five NBC network O and O's (the stations owned and operated by NBC in New York, Chicago, Cleveland, Los Angeles, and Washington). "We went to the big New York banks with our proposal and a request for loans," an associate of the Howard group reports, "but they turned us down." Among other things, the bankers suggested that there be

40 percent white representation on the board of directors
of the proposed company. At any time, a number of individual stations may be for sale around the country.
WOR-TV, the New York City station owned by RKO,
was available for about $60 million in the early 1970s;
the price has dropped sharply since, reflecting not only
the uncertain economic situation but also the realization
that it would cost several million dollars to overhaul
WOR's anemic news and public affairs programming initially, and more millions each year in order to make a
nonnetwork station competitive in the crowded New
York market.

Cable Fables

At $40 million, WOR is still an expensive proposition.
Some black communications specialists have considered
bypassing over-the-air television entirely and concentrat-
ing their ownership efforts in the cable television field.
Theodore S. Ledbetter, Jr., of the Urban Communications Group, Washington, D.C., speculates that the economics and politics of cable television may be more man-
ageable for the outs who want to get in. Cable franchises
will be awarded to some extent by city councils and by
mayors, and blacks can expect to have relatively more
leverage in certain cities. Also, cable television offers multiple channels, 24 or 48 at a minimum in the advanced
systems, which means that each city could permit parallel
ownerships and operations. In a city like Boston, the
black community of Roxbury could be connected by
cable without infringing on similar arrangements for the
Italian-Americans of the North End or the middle class of
the Back Bay. With the fragmenting of the cable TV

audience, of course, advertising revenues would be frag-
mented—and so would the money needed for programming. The vicious circle works like this: lack of money
for program production means poor advertising revenues,
which means lack of money. Some advocates of cable
television have argued that there are other potential
sources of income—the cable installation charge, sub-
scriber fees, revenues from cable services such as meter-
ing or banking—that are independent of advertisers. A
"position paper" written in 1972 by a black communications group discussed the prospect for black control of
cable television in these terms:

Jobs will be created for black film makers, producers,
directors, entertainers, writers, et al. Jobs connected with
the installation, manufacturing and repair of cable equipment will rapidly come into being. Through ownership
and utilization of its own channels of communication,
the black community will be able to take long strides in
education for both children and adults, in improved communications with local and federal organizations and in
developing the ethnic concept.[5]

By 1974, the group itself no longer existed, and the
cable industry as a whole was tempering its optimistic
projections. The dominant white-owned MSOs (Multiple Systems Operators) like Teleprompter and Time-Life
Broadcasting, suffered serious financial losses when new
cable subscribers failed to sign up at predicted rates of
growth. Because of the lack of strong financial resources
in black communities, many of the advocates of cable
television had begun to believe that the best route to
minority ownership of cable systems lay through the Internal Revenue Service regulations. A limited partnership
corporation, for example, would permit black community

groups to retain voting control of a cable operation while providing investment opportunities to wealthy whites with a conscience, and a need for tax shelters. As the glow dimmed for cable television, the tax shelter idea all but collapsed.

The Uses of Pressure

In the late 1960s and early 1970s, direct attempts were made to change broadcasting's "big blackout." The Communications Law provides that television station broadcast licenses be granted for three years of operation in the public convenience and interest. License challenges before the Federal Communications Commission and, equally important, the *threat* of license challenges became a popular method of leverage. The activities of Black Efforts for Soul in Television (BEST) were fairly typical. BEST helped secure a commitment from the Capital Cities Broadcasting Corporation to spend $1 million between 1972 and 1975 for "programming reflecting the perspective of black and Spanish-surnamed Americans." One of BEST's leaders was William Wright of Unity House, a Washington group funded by the Unitarian-Universalist Association. Wright attributed BEST's success with the broadcasters to its "strong negotiating position." Petitions to challenge the licenses of three Capital Cities stations (in Philadelphia, New Haven, Connecticut, and Fresno, California) were pending before the FCC at the time of the negotiations.

The Capital Cities agreement was frequently cited as an example of how a small group of private citizens could, in the words of the Reverend Everett Parker of the Office of Communications, United Church of Christ, force social

changes even in "a giant and sophisticated industry."
Parker, a journalist before he entered the ministry, was
one of the "public interest" advocates who began prod-
ding the broadcasting industry in the 1960s; for a time,
he was to television licensing what Ralph Nader had been
to automobile safety. A Parker-style public interest operation against a broadcaster was planned in stages. The
first step was to equip some 50 to 100 people with Sony
television sets, handbooks, and time sheets to monitor
intensively the amount and kind of programming appearing on the local channel singled out for attention. If minority interest programming and community services
were notably absent, and if there were few black, brown,
or yellow faces on camera, then the citizen group would
enter into negotiation sessions with the management to
correct these conditions. If the negotiations didn't produce an agreement or an accommodation, then Parker
and his associates would join with a community group to
file a petition to deny the license renewal application. Between 1968 and 1973, field representatives of Parker's
Office of Communications were active in a dozen cities,
and on behalf of Chicano and Indian groups as well as
blacks. For a broadcaster, a license challenge meant, at a
minimum, unwanted publicity and attention in an image-
conscious business, and often the challengers didn't have
to move beyond stage two of their campaign. In the summer of 1971, for example, five Dallas–Fort Worth broadcasting stations reached a "model agreement" with a co-
alition of 17 area minority groups. Although Dallas–Fort
Worth is an area with significant black, Chicano, and Indian populations, the broadcast outlets have been tightly
held by conservative white newspaper interests. The

Dallas Morning News owned WBAP-TV; the *Dallas Times-Herald* (a subsidiary of the Los Angeles Times-Mirror Company) owned KDFW-TV; and the third station, WFAA-TV, was owned by Carter Publications. Yet these and other Dallas–Fort Worth stations agreed by 1973 to have 60 new jobs filled by qualified minority people, to "actively" seek blacks, Mexican-Americans, and American Indians in newsroom positions, to begin training programs and scholarships to help minority employees, and to start programming that would reflect "more accurately the diversity and ethnic variety" of Dallas–Fort Worth.

Under FCC rules, license renewals proceed regionally across the country. April 1, 1972, was the renewal date for Massachusetts's 11 television stations, and the Office of Communications asked the FCC to defer action on *all* Massachusetts station licenses pending a study of the number of minority group members—as well as women employed at the stations. Later that year, the expiration of broadcast licenses in the Northern California region produced a challenge to the three network affiliates in San Francisco—the Westinghouse-owned KPIX (CBS); KRON (NBC), owned by the *San Francisco Chronicle* interests; and KGO, owned and operated by ABC—and to KTVI, an independent station in Oakland owned by Cox Broadcasting (owners of the *Atlanta Journal and Constitution).*

What has been the practical result of all this activity? First of all, no commercial station had lost its license as of this writing (the fall of 1974), and none seemed likely to lose its license. In fact, Congress was considering a bill that would increase the licensing period from three years to five years and also place a heavier burden on challengers.

Second, government figures show that the broadcast industry currently employs proportionately *fewer* minority group members in professional jobs than most other major industries in the United States. The precise figures on minority employment in broadcasting have been difficult to obtain, though in theory they should be readily available. Both the Federal Communications Commission and the Equal Employment Opportunity Commission require broadcast organizations to file employment information reports annually, but both commissions have been lax in processing and publishing this information. The EEOC was supplying only its 1969 figures well into 1972. Plain embarrassment may explain this laggard behavior. Extrapolating from the official figures and from some more current private studies, I estimated minority employment in broadcasting as of September 1974 at about 10 percent of the total broadcast work force of 140,000. (After I wrote this passage, the FCC released its official figures; see Sources and Notes, page 253.) Fourteen thousand is not an impressive number—except in contrast to the figures of the 1950s or 1960s—and the broadcasters often must move their minority journalists around quickly, like Foreign Legionnaires running from firing port to firing port at some besieged fort, in order to create the illusion of large numbers.

Finally, the supply of those able-bodied foot soldiers may be shut off. Between 1968 and 1974, the minority summer program of the Graduate School of Journalism at Columbia University recruited and trained 225 blacks, Orientals, and Spanish-surnamed Americans and placed them in journalism jobs. The program was discontinued after the summer session of 1974, when both the

television networks and the Ford Foundation withdrew
support (in the seven years of the program's operation,
the Ford Foundation had given some $1.5 million).
Robert C. Maynard of the *Washington Post,* the program's
last summer director, commented at the time, "by ending
the project, we are telling our minorities that the only
way to get things done is by rioting" (in mid-1975, a new
program was being developed at Berkeley).

Color-Blind?
Charlayne Hunter of the *New York Times* observed to me
during a discussion that black reporters were brought in
during the "heat of crisis"—as she was—and, as the crisis
seemed to subside, found themselves the "low men and
women on the totem pole." "We were brought in for a
special purpose; we have special problems." Among other
problems, she points out, black reporters say they are seldom called on to do the in-depth assignments or the in-
terpretive and analytical stories that could give younger
journalists in print and broadcasting a chance to build a
reputation. "You can't get assignments unless you have
experience," she says, "and you can't get experience unless you get assignments. And so they languish in the
newsrooms like The Spook Who Sat by the Door."

Young white reporters will recognize the complaint; the
institutional habits of the press are color-blind. At broadcast stations where management, for strictly licensing
reasons or out of a wider sense of responsibility, has made
sustained efforts to hire, train, and promote more than
one highly visible, token nonwhite, the specific benefits
have been tangible. Where there are three or more black
reporters and technicians at a station, they often take

their lunches or coffee breaks together—much like the "black tables" that have become common at university and college dining halls. But the goal is not social integration; if it happens, that is fine. The more important objective is the shaping of the product of the institution—collaboration in the "small" matters that determine the daily play of the news. Over a period of one week at one Washington television station, the following events took place:

—A white assignment editor sent a black reporter to cover a black community meeting; the reporter's story included the information that the "black national anthem" was sung at the meeting. The editor had not known that there *was* a black national anthem, nor did any of his white staff people; their listeners found out that evening (the anthem is called "Lift Every Voice and Sing").

—The day that the convict George Jackson was killed in a California prison, black reporters helped whites to judge the prison officials' claim that Jackson was able to conceal a handgun in his Afro-styled hair.

—White and black students had a "confrontation" at a suburban Maryland high school, attracting wide attention. The episode was covered by a black reporter and a white cameraman; the film was edited by the reporter together with a white news director. The result, on the 6:00 P.M. news that evening, was both clear and "balanced."

These changes in the daily atmosphere, desirable as they are, do not substantially modify the general climate of the institution. They do not change the definitions of what constitutes "news" and what does not; they do not affect the rhetorical conventions of the news, such as the "dramatic" model of conflict and resolution; the narrative point of view remains unchanged, as do the "acceptable" forms of argument and proof. In 1972, the National Black Political Convention was held in Gary, Indiana, the first such gathering of black Americans. Well over 100 men and women journalists, the majority black, were on hand to cover the convention. The amount of air time and print space given the proceedings around the country was modest. The stories that did appear tended to be the short "spot news" items. Several accounts emphasized conflict, "controversy," and disagreement between various black leaders at the convention. A sense of the historical "aura" of the meeting was missing in the stories and television accounts of the black reporters. A common complaint of the delegates was that the news reports failed to convey adequately the long planning and hard work that went into the meeting. The contributions of Imamu Baraka (formerly known as LeRoi Jones), who served as one of the convention organizers, went largely unreported. The major news of the convention, to judge by the weekend coverage, was the dramatic "split" between vying leaders Richard Hatcher, the mayor of Gary, and the Reverend Jessie Jackson of Chicago. It was the standard "dramatic" journalistic story form: tired, hackneyed, and (this time) black.

The normal institutional requirements explain why the convention was badly covered. The meetings didn't get started properly until late on a Saturday afternoon, a time inconvenient for the deadlines of the national networks, the newsmagazines, and the early-closing Sunday newspapers. The developing ITT case, the continuing Clifford Irving saga, and the final days of the Democratic Party presidential primary in Florida dominated the news that weekend. Many editors, creatures of habit, are at home with standard media events like the primaries—there were, in all, 23 presidential primaries in 1972—but profess to be lost with a story like the National Black Convention, except to treat it "traditionally." "We had a reporter and a crew out there," a CBS network television vice-president told me when I inquired about the poor coverage a few days after the convention ended. "But they didn't get much. The convention was a very disorganized affair. . . ."

The Spook by the Door

And so, as Charlayne Hunter says, good young men and women languish by the door. Discouragingly, many may not walk in the door at all. In the early 1970s, a number of campus surveys indicated that very few young black students appeared to be interested in becoming journalists. The predominantly black colleges across the country offered almost no journalism training. And in my own experience at two elite "white" schools, the black students I have talked to spoke of service to their "Brothers and Sisters back in the community." This usually translated into "serious" academic courses and activist career choices, such as law, planning, medicine, urban studies, and politics, rather than the more "passive" role of the journalist observer. Until the Watergate scandals and the work done by Carl Bernstein and Robert Woodward, it was hard to tell young blacks that they were wrong. Now, post-Watergate, I personally am seeing more young black men and women who want to work on newspapers or in television news—but not that many more.

Chapter 9
Psychojournalism: Nixon on the Couch

In the summer and fall of 1973, as the Watergate scandals propelled Richard Nixon into his seventh and most serious crisis, the state of the President's mental health became a national "issue." At least, the media made the President's mood and emotional well-being a prime subject of discussion. How much longer, many stories asked, could Richard Nixon "take the pressure"? His closest associates were falling one by one, and the vise of disclosure and evidence was tightening around him; would he "crack"? Indeed, had he *already* cracked?

These questions, in turn, created honest public apprehensions. The President's health is, obviously, a fit subject for public concern and serious discussion. Gene Smith in his excellent 1964 study of Woodrow Wilson, *When the Cheering Stopped,* described the tragedy of a President whose incapacity was shielded from the public by his family and the palace guard. And A. J. Liebling, in *The Earl of Louisiana,* showed how difficult it can be to remove a visibly sick official—in this case, Louisiana Governor Earl Long—even when his family and close aides lend a hand. A few years ago, the U.S. Congress, mindful of such experiences (as well as of Eisenhower's series of physical incapacities) provided a remedy of sorts in Section 4 of the Twenty-Fifth Amendment, which states that the vice-president and a majority of the Cabinet may, at any time, declare the president "unable to discharge the powers and duties of his office."

The Nixon White House, during late 1973 and early

1974, took the position that there was no "health story." Mr. Nixon himself maintained in an October 1973 news conference that "the tougher it gets, the cooler I get. . . ." He vowed to stay in office "as long as I am physically able" and coupled that statement with the information that he was working 16 to 18 hours a day. At the daily White House briefings, Gerald Warren, the assistant press secretary, regularly reassured reporters that the President was as fit as ever. One morning, I wrote down this exchange:

Question: Why does the President spend so much time at Camp David?
Warren: He finds it conducive to work.
Question: Does that mean that the President sleeps better at Camp David?
Warren: If you're trying to get me to say that the President doesn't sleep well in the White House, my reply is, he always sleeps well. . . .

But if the White House was practically opaque in its answers to the questions about the President's "mental state," the press was frustratingly elliptical in what it was willing to share with its audience. Many news accounts in the period between July 1973 and January 1974 engaged in a form of mass noncommunication that can only be called psychojournalism. The psychojournalistic style combines the worst side of speculative reporting with the most glib "insights" of pop psychology. The overall tone raises apprehensions without explicitly confronting them. In fact, having made the President's "mood" a matter of national concern during the last half of 1973, the President's analysts in the press then walked away from their patient. At the very end, however, the psychojournalists were around again, practicing analysis-at-a-distance.

HE STIGMA OF THERAPY . . . THE

The most serious offenders were the two major newsmagazines. The newsweekly habit of packaging events into
dramatic story form led to vivid passages like this *Time*
account of Mr. Nixon at a Veterans of Foreign Wars
appearance in New Orleans during the summer of 1973:

He said nothing for a few seconds, as if he were not sure
what to do. When he realized it was his turn to speak, he
turned his back to the audience, made an exaggerated,
impressario-like bow to the guests on stage, and fairly
bounded to the lectern. Occasionally, as he spoke, he
slurred his words or mispronounced them. His animated
gestures sometimes seemed to be unconnected with his
speech.

Or this from *Newsweek*'s national affairs department in
the issue of December 17, 1973:

Mr. Nixon's introversion and the visible erosion he now
shows when he does get out have fed the pervasive gossip
around Washington as to whether he is in danger of crack-
ing under the strain. . . . In this atmosphere it was noted,
and talked about, that his voice trembled badly when he
introduced his new energy man, Simon; that he had diffi-
culty fumbling the caps back onto pens he used at a bill-
signing ceremony; that he looked ashy at some of his
Operation Candor audiences and thickly made up at
others; that, by one account, he drained three highballs in
sixteen minutes before a White House dinner last week
and chased them with two quick glasses of wine at table.

In the cosmos of the newsweeklies, of course, people
"bound" rather than "walk." But "to drain a glass" con-
veys a quite different meaning than "to drink" or "to
sip." How much of this is the writer's hyperbole, and how
much is reality? And beyond the superheated style, there
are the preconceptions that the newsmagazine writer
brings to the story; the prose raises the question of

LETON CASE . . . THE NIXON CAS

whether the writer actually witnessed what was described or was "improving" on someone else's account. After reading *Time*'s account of the President's appearance at the VFW meeting, one medical man commented, "slurred speech, odd motions, missed words . . . They're describing the symptoms of a paranoid schizophrenic—without saying so!"

The wire services and the newspapers, less committed to the story-as-drama form and the "why" of events, were somewhat less guilty of practicing psychojournalism without a license—though not much less. Many of them, possessed of the same mind set, had to make do with the daily material at hand. Thus, in New Orleans, when the President gave Ronald Ziegler a shove, it became a page one sensation. The President has lost his temper! A cartoon by Don Wright of the *Miami News* showed Mr. Nixon picking up Ziegler and throwing him at the newspeople—a visual representation of the hyperbolic prose stories. And in Orlando, Florida, a few weeks later, the President first misidentifies an Air Force sergeant ("Are you this boy's mother or grandmother?") and then taps the sergeant's face. Suddenly, the story (Was it a slap? A resounding slap? Did the television lights temporarily blind the President? Or was some deeper force at work?) echoes around the world. The episode had been so trivial that the experienced reporters who witnessed it did not bother to put it in their files. Others, however, seized upon it as another symptom for the psychojournalistic case files.

The voice is passive, the language euphemistic, the confrontation with reality never direct. Apparently, the press is scattering clues around—it has some suspicions about

. . . PSYCHOHISTORY AND REDUC

Richard Nixon's "mental capacities"—but it doesn't have the courage (or the knowledge) to say so. The stories of these episodes hung in midair, feeding the public fears that something might be wrong. After five months of such locutions, the *New York Times,* in an otherwise well-balanced story, was still using code words:

For some time, Mr. Nixon's health and morale, and the motives behind his words and actions, have been a topic at Washington social gatherings, in conversations on Capitol Hill, in the departments and even in a number of White House offices.

It could be argued that Richard Nixon's notorious inaccessibility to reporters helped create the conditions under which speculation about his "health and morale" flourished. The Nixon White House's press relations made factual reporting of even the most rudimentary sort extremely difficult. Mr. Nixon never established any easy availability for the press, and after the Watergate deluge he became even more isolated and remote—and therefore a target of speculation. At the high tide of the Nixon years, between November 1972 and March 1973, he granted three private interviews to reporters. His news conferences tapered off to seasonal affairs—one every three or four months. The White House press regulars, a core of perhaps 40 to 50 men and women reporters, were reduced to seeking close-up glimpses of Mr. Nixon during his public appearances and in the routine "photo opportunities" arranged for the media before ceremonial meetings. According to the testimony of Bonnie Angelo, *Time* magazine's White House correspondent, "We could go for weeks without really seeing him."[1] Nor were the President's men any help in the last year before resignation.

NISM . . . THE QUEEG SCENARIO

Questions about the President's personal "feelings"—let alone his emotional well-being—were effectively stone-walled. A sick Richard Nixon entered Bethesda Naval Hospital on July 12, 1973, right after John Dean's devastating testimony before the Ervin committee. Later, at a news conference, Dr. Walter Tkach, the President's personal physician, diagnosed the trouble as pneumonia; when Dr. Tkach was asked by reporters if the President's condition was the result of worry or overwork, the doctor blandly replied, "Anyone can suffer viral pneumonia . . ." *(New York Times,* July 13, 1973). Only much later did the word get out that General Alexander Haig, the White House chief of staff, was telling some people privately that Mr. Nixon had been "coughing blood before going to Bethesda . . ." (*Newsweek,* December 3, 1973).

The need to present the President in the best possible light is an accepted part of White House public relations. For example, John F. Kennedy used a sunlamp for cosmetic purposes, and there was an unwritten rule against photographing FDR in his wheelchair. But the handling of the Nixon "health issue" by both the White House and the press goes deeper into the dark soil of American attitudes about mental health and mental illness.

The Stigma of Therapy
It is a political truism that no national politician—still, today—can survive with the burden of an emotional illness in his medical history. All of the White House noncomments and opacities about Richard Nixon's well-being become perfectly clear once this is understood. This is the case even though mental disturbance may be the second most common medical complaint after the common cold

in American life. Theodore White observes in his account
of the events that led to the removal of Senator Thomas
Eagleton from the Democratic ticket in 1972: "American
folklore had not yet learned to separate the degrees and
different natures of mental illness."[2] White locates this
attitude among older Americans; in the Heartland, away
from the sophisticated cities, psychotherapy constitutes
a "stigma" too strong to shake. "It is safer for a politician
to go to a whorehouse than to see a psychiatrist," Dr.
Arnold Hutschnecker told a *Washington Post* reporter
during the period of intense speculation about Richard
Nixon's health. " . . . I can't be seen within a diameter of
the White House. At this time, they would say 'ah ha.'
. . ."[3] Dr. Hutschnecker was his own best example of his
argument. All stories about him—including the *Washington
Post*'s—meticulously pointed out that Dr. Hutschnecker
had Richard Nixon as a patient *before* he shifted his
practice from internal medicine to psychotherapy in the
mid-1950s. Dr. Hutschnecker's name also came up during
the Senate committee hearings on the nomination of
Gerald Ford for Vice-President in the fall of 1973. As
Linda Charlton's excellent account in the *New York
Times* explained, "One question kept recurring, from
members of both parties, for which no rationale was advanced, and none was immediately apparent. The question, phrased one way or another, concerned allegations
that, five or six years ago, Mr. Ford was treated by Dr.
Arnold Hutschnecker. . . ." Ford was able to calm the
senators' apprehensions. It turned out that *Mrs.* Ford was
the one in the family who had "seen a psychiatrist."
When the Fords moved into the White House, the "color"
stories on Betty Ford carefully included the fact that she

still took daily tranquilizers. "Twenty-five years of being both housewife and House wife has left its scars on Betty Ford," *Newsweek* reported in its August 19, 1974, issue— "and she is quick to admit it. For the last nine years, while her husband held the hectic, day-and-night job of House Minority Leader, she was left almost single-handed to cope with their then adolescent children. She developed psychosomatic pains, turned to psychiatry and tranquillizers (which she still uses daily) and even made her husband promise to quit politics after the next election."

The Eagleton Case

It is also a fact of life that the national press corps, largely urban, educated, and moderately well read, understands more about mental illness than does Middle America— but not much more. Once that is accepted, the peculiar métier of psychojournalism also becomes perfectly clear. The case of Senator Thomas Eagleton of Missouri is instructive. On Tuesday, July 25, 1972, just two weeks after the Democratic National Convention, Tom Eagleton, the man selected by Senator George McGovern as his running mate on the Democratic presidential ticket, held a news conference in a resort lodge in the Black Hills of South Dakota, where McGovern had been resting before the campaign. Two reporters for the Knight Newspapers, Robert Boyd and Clark Hoyt, had established that Eagleton had three times been hospitalized for mental disorders. Brit Hume, at the time an associate of the syndicated columnist Jack Anderson, described what happened at the meeting:

With the Knight papers poised to break the story, Eagleton and McGovern decided to make a public confession

immediately. Eagleton's statement to a roomful of stunned
reporters contained assurances that he was fully recovered,
that his problem had been "nervous exhaustion" and that
he had learned to "pace" himself so that he would not
have the problem again. Nevertheless, he acknowledged
that he had undergone electric-shock treatment on two of
the occasions when he had been hospitalized. There could
be no doubt that it was a devastating development for the
Democratic ticket. Eagleton was an attractive and articu-
late man, considered a remarkably talented politician by
his colleagues. But would the public place a man with a
history of mental illness a heartbeat from the presidency?
Most people doubted it. The headlines the next morning
were very large.[4]

Eagleton tried to stay on the ticket. Early in his ordeal
he said he hoped to use all the attention he was getting
"to educate people about mental illness. . . ." The effort
was received with some sympathy, initially, by many newspeople. Some commentators thoughtfully pointed out
the possibility that a man or woman willing to begin the
unsparing self-examination inherent in psychiatric psychotherapy might be a person of both courage and intelligence—and might emerge from the therapy a "healthier"
personality than the leader who grimly refuses to enter-
tain the idea that some form of therapy might, under
certain conditions, be of enormous help. But the fact that
Eagleton had undergone electroshock treatment was ultimately decisive for the more knowing. Theodore White
summed up this "sophisticated" view when he observed
that a Strategic Air Command pilot or a nuclear sub-
marine captain would be removed from command with
the medical history of a Tom Eagleton.

In truth, the Eagleton "case" was closed from the beginning. At the first South Dakota news conference,

literally hundreds of pictures were taken. But one UPI picture made the first page of newspapers across the country the next day: the one photo showing Eagleton "nervously" patting his head. Eagleton himself was to complain bitterly that he couldn't beat the selection system. "During the entire time I kept my head up," he said, in describing another encounter, "but just once I lowered my head and that's the shot they all used. . . ." In an appearance on CBS's "Face the Nation" program, Eagleton handled himself extremely well—only to have a "helpful" CBS correspondent, George Herman, observe that the viewer may have noticed that the Senator was perspiring heavily and had a slight "tremor." There was some sweat on Eagleton's forehead—the studio lights were hot—but not many home television sets could have picked up the "tremor." He was no more or no less shaky than any of his interrogators, including Herman.

The Eagleton strategy to counteract the impression of his unfitness was to be highly visible, to stay in the public eye instead of canceling appearances ("See, he's in hiding, he can't take the pressure. . ."). But Eagleton's round of activities—San Francisco to Hawaii to Washington—served to keep the story moving by providing fresh datelines and new camera angles. His movement contributed to the atmosphere that eventually undid him.

The Nixon Case

Richard Nixon received another sort of psychojournalistic treatment. In the Eagleton case, there was a tangible record of hospitalization to play against; by Richard Nixon's own testimony, he has never had so much as a headache in all his life. The reasonably "sophisticated" journalist,

upon hearing that, would say—as several did—*Ah ha! He's
denying it all. He's overly rigid!* In this case the journalist's
pop knowledge of psychiatry may undermine genuine
understanding as much as Middle America's massive ignorance. A little knowledge can be a dangerous thing.

Still, a large number of White House reporters resisted
making such diagnoses.[5] "I don't think I should speculate
about the President's mental health," Ford Rowan, the
White House correspondent for Television News, Inc.
(TVN), told me about the time the psychojournalistic
analyses were appearing. "That's not my job. If President
Nixon did something bizarre, like shoving Ziegler, I'd report it, but that's all. . . ." The pressure on the reporters
may come from bureau chiefs or editors in New York
who believe, apparently, that they are on top of the workings of the human psyche ("The rigid personalities really
crack after a while. . ."). One newsmagazine reporter
recalls that the story queries from her editors in New York
"wanted to know what drugs was the President taking . . .
what were the dosage levels . . . was he on 'uppers' at his
Disney World news conference. . . ." It was, she said,
"just utter nonsense. . . ."

Another reporter, Saul Pett of the Associated Press,
wrestled for weeks with an assignment on "the President's
mood." He finally asked himself, "Am I qualified to do
this?" His own answer was: Probably not. (Yet, in good-
soldier fashion, he slogged his way through an elliptical
story.) The essential question is one of qualification. It is
difficult to see exactly on what basis the journalist, even
the well-schooled journalist, can judge personality and
behavior, especially in a figure as inaccessible as Richard
Nixon was during his presidency. Over the last decade, it

is true, a small group of psychiatrists, political scientists, and historians have developed lively methods of applying Freudian psychoanalytic principles to such political leaders as de Gaulle, Bismarck, and Gandhi. The political scientist James David Barber and the historian Bruce Mazlish have extended the idea to American presidents, including Richard Nixon.[6] But psychohistory remains more an art than a science; the professionals are still learning how to do it.

Psychohistory and Reductionism
At times, as the better psychohistorians are the first to admit, the psychiatric analysis of political figures can sound ridiculous. Psychohistorians often foolishly engage in what Mazlish calls reductionism—stripping a political figure down to his oral, genital, and anal aspects. At times, too, the psychiatric profession has been guilty of plain bad judgment. In 1964, Ralph Ginsberg's magazine *Fact* solicited the membership of the American Psychiatric Association for its views on the mental health of presidential candidate Barry Goldwater. A majority of those replying held Goldwater to be "unfit" for the presidency. Dr. Lester Grinspoon, a Cambridge psychiatrist who has written about the pressures on political leaders, refused to get involved in the "survey." "These doctors," he says, "never spent a minute with Goldwater even to shake his hand and they are describing him as a 'paranoid.'. . ."

The Queeg Scenario
Practiced by journalists, psychological analysis-at-a-distance can be disastrous. Perhaps one of the best cases for more frequent televised, live presidential news conferences

has been made by the Washington correspondent Peter Lisagor, who argues that they give the public a chance to see "the demeanor of the President" as the press tests him. Appearances can be deceptive, however, and the interpretation of this "demeanor" is subject to some serious limitations.

First of all, standards of judgment often are subjective. The television networks can let the camera do the "psychological" reporting for them; print people have to put it into words. After President Nixon faced the press at an October 26, 1973, news conference, the front-page story in the *New York Times* reported that the President looked "fatigued," while the analysts on the inside pages described him as looking "healthy and vigorous." Two Associated Press correspondents who were in the room couldn't agree on the right description either: one man thought he looked "cool"; the other, "out of control." If it seems so hard to judge outward appearances, what then can be said of inward feelings?

Richard Nixon remained very much the master of his own public "demeanor" as long as he was in the White House. Much of the psychojournalism about him reflected basic misconceptions of personality and of emotional control. Perhaps the most common notion—fed by motion picture images of Captain Queeg and the courtroom behavior of television characters—is that a witness often "breaks" under heavy pressure or skillful cross-examination. The Long Island newspaper *Newsday* actually ran a long article likening the President's behavior during Watergate to Queeg's behavior on the *Caine*—accompanied by matching pictures of Richard Nixon and Humphrey Bogart. In life, if not in art, most successful adults who "function" in the public eye have long since worked out ways to handle their private struggles. The neutral word that psychiatrists use for this is "adaptation."

Those viewers who waited for one of the Watergate witnesses to "crack" under dramatic, hammering questions had a long wait. Similarly, no Perry Mason of the press was able to "break" the President on live television. Yet the notion persisted that just one more blow would crack Richard Nixon's composure; the picture of the besieged and battered President had been painted so grimly that some readers could not be blamed for expecting the man to be carted away momentarily.

Fortunately, a kind of self-corrective mechanism eventually took over. One can carry around the sign proclaiming "The End of the World Is at Hand" for only so long. Despite all the rumors and gossip-as-news through the period of the Watergate revelations, there was no evidence that Richard Nixon had "cracked"—and ample evidence that he had his wits about him. Naturally, he was under enormous stress; anyone with the plumbers, ITT, Howard Hughes, the milk fund, income taxes, the Houston plan, San Clemente, Key Biscayne, Bebe Rebozo, and the missing tapes on his mind could not help but look ravaged and find it hard to sleep. But when a few newspapers like the *Washington Post* and the *New York Times* finally called in some expert witnesses for an opinion, they were told, as Bruce Mazlish wrote in the *Post,* that no one should expect any sudden or dramatic "breaks" in the Nixon personality. Or as the psychiatrist Lester Grinspoon observed, "Contrary to all the talk about crackups, there is a great *stability* and *consistency* about Nixon; he has been behaving now exactly the same as in his whole public life. . . ."

As a result of such straightforward and legitimate psychojournalism by qualified people, the cut-rate brand of diagnosis went out of fashion for a time. The medical calls in the media ceased, for a while, and reporters had to face the drearier task of covering the day-to-day business of how the stable, consistent Nixon—the *Old* Nixon—was trying to run the country.

The respite lasted until the end of April, when the release of the White House tapes produced another manic round of analysis. This time, a modicum of the personal materials that the psychohistorian needs was available. Reflecting a popular judgment, the British journalist Peter Jenkins called the tapes "an authentic encounter with the private Nixon" and, pushing psychojournalism to a logical extreme, said that the tapes raised a question about the "President's mentality, indeed, his rationality. . . ." "What if, after all, he is a psychopath?" Jenkins asked in *New York* magazine. Jenkins never wholly answered his own question; he doesn't clearly define what kind of psychopathology he is talking about (except to misuse the word "schizophrenia" when he plainly means "schizoid personality"). But Jenkins leaves no doubt in which direction he thinks the evidence tilts. The psychojournalists, who had obliquely worried about the President's "mood" in the summer of 1973, were in the summer of 1974 openly proclaiming his "madness"—on the basis of 33 hours of edited, selective conversations.

It is, of course, easier to play doctor to Richard Nixon than to subject the office of the presidency to serious, steady analysis on a regular basis. But it is not merely a case of journalists being lazy, or irresponsible, or both. Journalists do not tend to think in institutional terms; they tend to reject organizational explanations of behavior—their own especially—in favor of idiosyncratic explanations. As a result, the office of the presidency, as opposed to the particular president in office, largely goes unexamined. During the first weeks of the Gerald Ford presidency, for example, we all learned how the new chief executive toasted his English muffins, but not how he made decisions. Eight months later, the television screens were devoting as much time to his "trick knee"—which caused him to stumble in Austria getting off his airplane— as to his European diplomacy.

Chapter 10
**The White House: What Did the Press Know?
When Did the Press Know It?**

In late March 1973, when the Watergate cover-up was beginning to come unstuck, White House Press Secretary Ronald Ziegler announced that President Nixon was ordering members of his staff to appear before the Watergate grand jury and to testify, if summoned. The *Washington Star* promptly reported the announcement as a significant change of policy: Nixon was relaxing his stand on executive privilege in order to cooperate with the investigation. At the *Washington Post,* the national affairs desk picked up and reported substantially the same theme, despite the strenuous protests of the paper's two Watergate men, Carl Bernstein and Robert Woodward.[1] They objected—correctly, it turned out—that the "new policy" was nothing more than a public relations gesture, an attempt to create the appearance of cooperation with the grand jury—whose deliberations were both secret and under the control of the Administration's Justice Department—while at the same time stonewalling the *open, independent* hearings of the Senate Watergate Committee.

Recalling that particular Ziegler feint—and the press's tumble—in their book, *All the President's Men,* Woodward and Bernstein observe that "Nine months after Watergate, the White House demonstrated once again that it knew more about the news business than the news business knew about the White House."

The episode was a relatively small crosscurrent in the huge torrent of Watergate; but the Woodward-Bernstein verdict about the overall performance of the news business was resoundingly confirmed—like so much else of the two reporters' work—by subsequent events. Indeed, the depressing evidence of just how little the news business knows of the White House's business—still—can be judged by the press's treatment of the edited volume of tape-recorded presidential conversations submitted to the House Judiciary Committee on April 30, 1974. The proper full title is *Submission of Recorded Presidential Conversations to the Committee of the Judiciary of the House of Representatives by President Richard Nixon* (Washington: U.S. Government Printing Office, 1974). The popular short title is *The White House Tapes.*

Quantitatively, the press did a superb job in handling the sheer bulk of the White House tapes.[2] In Chicago, the *Tribune* had a word-for-word supplement of the text for sale on newsstands the morning after the document was made public. The National Public Radio staff read on the air, in uninflected style, all of the published transcriptions—which the White House said encompassed 33 hours of conversation; the reading took about 22 hours, which hints at the magnitude of what was labeled "material unrelated to presidential action," "characterization deleted," "inaudible," and "unintelligible." NBC News and CBS News both offered highlights from the tapes, NBC with professional readers taking the roles of P, D, E, and H, and CBS with correspondents reading the passages. An Associated Press survey estimated that no fewer than 25 newspapers had run off the full texts by mid-May. Everyone soon had a favorite citation; some of the most notorious lines were set in Haiku form.

The quality of the transcript coverage, however, was another matter. Set before publishers and broadcast

TAPE SHOCK . . . "GUILTY, GUIL

executives the technical challenge of getting out information, and they perform admirably. *Editor and Publisher* magazine noted with admiration that the 300,000-plus words in the transcripts constituted "the longest item [United Press International] has ever transmitted. . . ." But ask for the needed analysis and interpretation, and the wires go limp.

Tape Shock

Overall, the press response to the White House transcripts was one of self-professed shock, surprise, and moral outrage. A good part of this response involved the straight reporting of the words of public figures, such as Senator Hugh Scott of Pennsylvania, a Nixon supporter who called the transcripts "deplorable, disgusting, shabby, immoral." But there were also exegesis and comment. *Newsweek,* for example, described the edited transcripts as "a brutally revealing glimpse into the sort of *realpolitik* practiced by Mr. Nixon. . . ." The *Chicago Tribune* said, simply, "We have seen the private man, and we are appalled."

Fair enough. Yet an equally warranted reaction could just as properly be one of embarrassment. In all the hand-wringing—over the "amorality" of the Nixon gang—and in all the mutual stroking—over the press's role in exposing the low life of the Oval Office—the essential deficiency of the national press itself went relatively unremarked. Richard Nixon had been a public man for 28 years when the transcripts were released; realpolitik has been practiced by presidents as long as there has been the Republic; and swearing, Ashley Montagu assures us, is "as old as man and coeval with language." Why, then, did the image

JILTY!". . . THE NIXON STYLE . . .

of politics in general, and Richard Nixon in particular,
apparently come as such a jarring revelation to the news
business? The columnist Joseph Alsop was a frequent
Nixon supporter, often speaking on the telephone with
the White House. Yet Alsop disconsolately wrote of the
tapes that the atmosphere was like "the backroom of a
second-rate advertising agency in a suburb of Hell." Where
had Alsop and the other political reporters and their editors been all the years that Richard Nixon was around?
What was the source of all the piety in the accounts of the
transcripts?

"Amoral" has probably been the most frequently used
description of the Nixon transcripts in the press's expli-
cations de texte. "Soul-less," "sleazy," and "insensitive"–
as in "appallingly insensitive to his moral obligations"–
are also high on the list of adjectives. Yet, when the Watergate break-in and cover-up story begins to point to John
Mitchell–"The Big Enchilada"–the transcripts (admitted-
ly edited by the White House) can be made to yield a
somewhat different picture of Richard Nixon. He may
have cunningly wanted to offer Mitchell as a sacrificial
lamb, but not without some sensitivity to his obligations.

First, there appears to be a genuine effort to find out
who did authorize–"sign off"–the Liddy intelligence plan.
From the March 21, 1973, meeting of Nixon and Dean:

D   . . .Liddy laid out a million dollar plan that was the
most incredible thing I've ever laid my eyes on: all in
codes, and involved black bag operations, kidnapping,
providing prostitutes to weaken the opposition, bugging,
mugging teams. It was just an incredible thing.

P   Tell me this: did Mitchell go along–?

D   No, no, not at all, Mitchell just sat there puffing and
laughing. . . .[3]

PRESS INNOCENCE . . . INCOMPET

Second, after sounding as if he really was trying to find out what happened, Nixon began facing the possibility that John Mitchell—his old law partner, campaign manager, and friend—might take the fall:

D . . . I was suggesting a meeting with Mitchell.

P . . . Now, Mitchell has to be there because he is seriously involved and we are trying to keep him with us. We have to see how we handle it from here on. We are in the process of having to determine which way to go. . . .

And this passage from a meeting on March 27:

E I say any idea of a meeting between you and Mitchell ought to wait until the Magruder, Haldeman, Mitchell meeting. . . .

P What about the other way around? How about me getting Mitchell in and say, look (unintelligible) you've got to tell us what the score is, John. You have to face up to where we are. What do you say? How do we handle (unintelligible)—

The President may want Mitchell to be as "high up as they've [the Watergate Committee] got." But this is hardly Humphrey Bogart telling Mary Astor, "I'm sending you over" to the cops.

Third, there is abundant evidence in the edited transcripts that Richard Nixon was trying to save his own skin; he and his lieutenants cast around, struggling in hopes of "containing" the scandal, "buying time," "reducing our losses," and "keeping the cap on the bottle." But there is also, as counterpoint, evidence of a concern about acting "presidential" and not prejudicing the rights of possible accused. From the meeting of March 21:

P . . .That is the proper way to do this. It should be done in the Grand Jury, not up there under the kleig lights of the Committee.

IN THE WHITE HOUSE . . . AND IN

There is also a passage in a midnight telephone conversation with John Ehrlichman on April 14, 1973, that can be read, if one chooses, as revealing a President trying to decide what is "right" as well as what is politic:

P   Fine. Well, John, you have had a hell of a week—two weeks. And of course poor Bob [Haldeman] is going through the tortures of the damned.

E   Yeah. That family thing is rough.

P   I know the family thing. But apart from the family thing, you know, he is a guy that has just given his life, hours and hours and hours, you know, totally selfless and honest and decent. That is another thing! Damn it to hell, I am just about to say. Well you know you get the argument of some, anybody that has been charged against, you should fire them. I mean you can't do that. Or am I wrong?

E   No, you are right.

P   Well, maybe I am not right. I am asking. They say, clean the boards. Well, is that our system?

E   Well that isn't a system. You know, that is a machine. That's—

P   That's right. I feel, honestly,—I mean, apart from the personal feelings we both have for Bob, don't you? But you know, I raised this myself. One way out is to say, well look, as long as all these guys have been charged, out they go and they can fight this battle and they can return when they get cleared. It is not good, is it?

E   You know I don't think it is. I don't think that is any way to run a railroad. I think—

P   Well, the point is, whatever we say about Harry Truman, etc., while it hurt him a lot of people admired the old bastard for standing by people—

E   Sure.

P   —who were guilty as hell—

E   Yep.

THE WHITE HOUSE PRESS CORPS

P —and damn it I am that kind of person. I am not one who is going to say, look, while this guy is under attack, I drop him. Is there something to be said for that, or not?

E I don't think, number one, I don't think you would gain anything by it. The problem doesn't go away.

P No, they will say, oh, that Nixon's top person, closest man to him, in the office four or five hours a day, and out he goes. Everything must be wrong!

E Yep—that is it. That is like separating Siamese twins.

"Guilty, Guilty, Guilty!"

True, this is not the swift, firm, cool decision making that Richard Nixon, in his book *Six Crises* and in his controlled interviews with selected reporters, would have us believe has characterized his personal and presidential style. And true, questions of tactics and appearance are raised. But neither is it the wholly craven behavior that the glosses put forward. The transcript coverage and commentary substituted one cardboard portrait for the older, one-dimensional figure with flag in lapel. Reality, as always, proves to be more complicated than art. The *New Republic* commentator TRB (Richard Lee Strout), perhaps the shrewdest of Washington observers, has pointed out that the transcripts should be read as a complicated drama. "It shouts for a Shakespeare," he wrote:

Who else could do justice to the crewcut Haldeman, the scowling Ehrlichman, the make-believe strong man Nixon, caught like the little ventriloquist from Kansas behind the throne in the Wizard of Oz? Or, above all, John W. Dean 3d, right out of Shakespeare's barrel of villains, young, supple, obsequious, fawning—the brightest one in the crowd, instantly adapting himself to the newest Nixon fantasy, saying when Nixon suggests he tell a cock-and-bull story to the Cabinet, that he will spin such a yarn as will astonish them.[4]

Instead of high theater, we were given cartoons. Literally. In May 1973, Gary Trudeau's brilliant Doonesbury strip, distributed by Universal Press Syndicate, carried Megaphone Mark Slackmeyer's radio commentary on Watergate:

It would be a disservice to [John] Mitchell and his character to prejudge the man, but everything known to date could lead one to conclude he's guilty.

And in the next panel, disc jockey Mark shouts into his microphone:

THAT'S GUILTY, GUILTY, GUILTY, GUILTY!

———

In May 1974, Megaphone Mark's shouts were echoed—about Mitchell, President Nixon, and the rest of the palace guard—in the reaction to the transcripts. There was much the same mixture of hypocrisy and certainty. Very few press people in Washington doubted that Nixon was "guilty"—of something, somehow. (And I include myself in this group.) But the hard evidence was not in the transcripts released on April 30. The "smoking gun"—the specific evidence of cover-up and obstruction of justice—finally appeared in early August, when Nixon surrendered, under court order, further tapes.

To raise questions about the press's coverage of the transcripts appears somewhat untimely and ill-mannered. Richard Nixon, after all, proved to be as guilty as he was prejudged to be. To accuse journalists of not being Shakespeares, when they have helped corral the Nixon Administration bad guys, seems terribly picky—like expecting Richard Nixon to sound like Lear rather than, well, the Richard Nixon of Checkers in 1952 and California in 1962.

The Nixon Style

In all the paper blizzard of text and exegesis, the basic legal issues that the House Judiciary Committee was seeking to determine when it subpoenaed the transcripts in the first place had become blurred. The questions were: Was the President involved in the Watergate break-in planning and/or cover-up? Did he authorize the payment of hush money? Did he encourage perjury? Did he obstruct justice? On these *substantive* issues both President and press were in agreement: the published transcripts of April 30 were incomplete, confusing, ambiguous. "Much depends on the eye of the beholder" (R. W. Apple, Jr.– *New York Times*).[5] "Parts may seem contradictory with one another" (Richard M. Nixon–speech to nation, April 29, 1974). All this may have been part of the White House "game plan," such as it was, of delay and deception. But the press, incredibly, was taken in by the last of the continuing cover-up tactics. The April 30 batch of tapes– edited, gapped, less than asked for by the committee– left the fundamental legal issues unresolved and underlined the need to get more tapes in unexpurgated form. Here was a clear issue that required a minimum of throat-clearing about "objectivity" and "fairness." But a press campaign to get more tapes released would have been "partisan." It would have meant *taking sides*– as if disclosure of evidence was a Democratic-Republican issue. Instead of a consistent and fervent crusade backing the House Judiciary Committee's demands for evidentiary substance, the press became preoccupied with the sideshow of the presidential style. Mr. Nixon was faulted for his language, for his rambles and short attention span, for his concern with public relations and image, for his obsession with scenario making—not only how it would play in Peoria but also how the newsmagazines might cover a specific development in the case, such as John Mitchell's involvement.

Though well documented, this is hardly an impressive list of crimes. The profanity and the slurs can shock only some Rip van Winkle who slept through the Truman, Eisenhower, Johnson, and Kennedy years. Even when the deleted expletives are filled in, it is mild enough stuff compared to, say, the conversations in newsmagazine editorial offices or a Radcliffe dorm. Of course, the Nixon constituency wasn't in New York or Cambridge but out in Middle America, where culturally, as the political scientist Walter Dean Burnham explains, "We are still an idealistic nation and where presidents aren't supposed to take the Lord's name in vain. . . ."[6] Also, it was Richard Nixon who came on so sanctimoniously in the 1960 campaign about Harry Truman's "bad" language; but press piety is no better than presidential piety.

We have also wallowed in the disjointed sentences, the interruptions, the lack of deference shown to the President by Messrs. Haldeman and Ehrlichman. But if digression is a crime, then Lyndon Johnson, even his admiring former aides say, would be guilty in the first degree. Group conversations, among professors of English literature, no less, usually sound incoherent when they are transcribed. A big-city mayor—liberal, attractive, intelligent—recently was inspired, if that is the word, by the Nixon transcripts to tape-record his own regular staff meeting and then play back the results to his surprised assistants. "First of all," he reports, "none of us would want any of our talk to get out in public. Second, we all came across like complete ninnies, although we *thought* we were making sense at the time. . . ."[7]

Press Innocence
Similarly, the media shock expressed at all the scenario making betrays a short memory of past kitchen cabinets, contingency planners, and crisis managers (and, further back, of the practical handbooks of Aristotle and Machiavelli). It also suggests a certain innocence about the practice of real politics. An aide to a leading politician—a certified "Mr. Clean"—says, "I can't remember a strategy meeting when we weren't all making scenarios." Another upper-level politician, who has run a large government bureaucracy, says, "There isn't a day that goes by that we weren't thinking—how will the newspapers play this? Will it make the six o'clock news? What will the party leaders say? How will our people react?" For a time, I believed that the press professions of distaste about the Nixon scenario building were mostly hypocritical; but an informal survey of a half-dozen political operatives convinced me that, as one said, "They [the reporters] simply have no true idea of what goes on inside. . . ." The habit of discursive, devious political talk is so ingrained—so "natural" for politicians—that it can't be kicked, even with the horrible example of the White House tapes to learn from. A few weeks after the tapes were released, a political acquaintance of mine telephoned an old friend, a governor who has national aspirations. After a 45-minute personal conversation, he mused, "That would kill him if it had been recorded. . . ." One value of the transcripts for

political reporters, as well as political scientists, is that they do permit outsiders to look inside; journalists and academicians are usually involved with the intellectual tasks of research, proof, and history, rather than the politician's task of *doing*. Action in politics requires consideration of political options.

Incompetents in the White House . . .
There is one description of Richard Nixon and his inner circle that is entirely warranted on the basis of the edited tapes: the word is "inept." Though they were advertising executives (H. R. "Bob" Haldeman, Ronald Ziegler) and lawyers (Nixon, John Ehrlichman, John Dean), the President and his men weren't even good at their own game of image making and presenting a competent brief. They didn't understand the operations of a grand jury or the rules of immunity; Mr. Nixon had to be instructed in the meaning of the term "unindicted co-conspirator." Only John Dean—"the brightest one"—seemed to know the law. The "PR side" isn't much better. What the tapes really reveal is not so much the extent of the Nixonian news management—every recent president has tried that—but the inability to control the PR. There is a lot of tough talk about making trouble for the Washington Post Company, for example, through pressure on its broadcast properties—but not much action or, rather, effective action.

In a conversation of September 15, 1972, omitted from the White House transcripts but released by the House Committee (which made its own transcripts from subpoenaed tapes), Nixon, Haldeman, and Dean discuss retaliation against the *Post* for its Watergate coverage:

P That's right. The main, main thing is The Post is going to have damnable, damnable problems out of this one. They have a television station—

D That's right, they do.

P —and they're going to have to get it renewed.

H They've got a radio station, too.

P Does that come up, too? The point is, when does it come up?

D I don't know. But the practice of nonlicensees filing on top of licensees has certainly gotten more—

P That's right.

D —more active in the, this area.

P And it's going to be God damn active here.

If the Nixon White House encouraged the Florida groups that challenged the *Post* stations in Miami and Jacksonville, they certainly chose poorly; one of the principals in one of the challenges subsequently became deeply entangled with the law for misappropriating hospital funds.

The point is not to play down the power of the FCC or the FBI in the hands of hardball players, to use a favorite White House phrase. But the transcripts show a largely unorganized pickup team of softballers. In one intriguing conversation, for example, the President and his men discuss leaking material to the press without directly involving the White House. Dean says he has obtained information from a former FBI official, William Sullivan, that President Johnson may have bugged Spiro T. Agnew's campaign plane and Anna Chennault in 1968; Dean suggests giving the information to *U.S. News & World Report.* The President offers several options, including a congres-

sional hearing: "Rather than going to a hearing to call
him [Sullivan]. That is quite the way to do it. Have him
give an interview to *U.S. News,* 'Wires in the Sky'. . . ."
Another suggestion was to give the story to Clark Mollen-
hoff, Washington bureau chief of the *Des Moines Register
and Tribune,* who had served as a presidential aide early
in the Nixon Administration. None of these ingenuous
options was tried.

. . . And in the White House Press Corps
Yet where in the world did we get the picture of the con-
summate political "pro" Richard Nixon? And the accompanying portraits of his smooth Teutonic staff that made
the executive office run on time? Where but from the
White House and the press? President Nixon kept telling
us how cool and savvy he was. Domestically, the Nixon
promise of a "new American Revolution" ceased to exist
even as a PR "talking point" in his first term. The great
international "triumphs" of the first term required not
only Henry Kissinger's talents but a decisive boost from
the Soviet Union. At least one Cabinet officer, long before
Watergate, privately sized up Nixon as a "make-believe
strongman" and used the Watergate paralysis to run his
own independent shop. Admiring newspaper profiles and
newsmagazine cover stories were touting "brilliant" Bob
Haldeman and "supercompetent" John Ehrlichman when
Republican associates could remember them only for their
ability to get the luggage in the lobby by 6:00 A.M. during
one or another of the Nixon campaigns.

    Richard Whalen, the former *Fortune* writer and author,
joined the Nixon campaign in 1968 but left early in the
first term, put off by the "buttoned-down scurrying

aides." In his 1972 book, *Catch a Falling Flag,* Whalen
quotes a White House official as saying:

Haldeman and Ehrlichman shield the President by mo-
nopolizing him. One of them is present at every meeting—
he sees no one alone. He has made himself their captive.
Sometimes the 'Germans' don't carry out Nixon's orders,
or they let papers sit on their desks for a while, because
they are certain he won't find out. How *can* he find out?
All the channels flow back to Haldeman.

Bob Haldeman usually stayed away from reporters, so
perhaps the press could plead a certain ignorance of the
man. But in early February 1972, he briefly surfaced on
the NBC "Today Show." Haldeman talked about the critics of the Nixon Administration's Vietnam policies. Before the President outlined all his peace plans, Haldeman
said, "you could say that his critics . . . were unconsciously
echoing the line that the enemy wanted echoed. Now,
after this [the President's] explanation," Haldeman continued, "after the whole activity is on the record and is
known, the only conclusion you can draw is that the critics now are consciously aiding and abetting the enemy of
the United States. . . ." The phrase "aiding and abetting
the enemy," of course, echoes the definition of treason.

Yet in the *Newsweek* cover story of March 19, 1973,
the tone is still admiring. For example, the magazine had
this to say about the leader of Mr. Nixon's "Palace Guard":

Haldeman's admirers, who include most of the people who
really matter in Richard Nixon's government, regard him
as a genius at a thankless trade—probably one of the best
ever. His old colleague John Mitchell calls him "a straight-
shooter . . . an all-American man in every sense of the
word"—a judgment and a vocabulary the President himself presumably shares, although, perhaps fittingly, he has

never made a public statement about Haldeman. He is diamond-bright (with a genius-range IQ) and diamond-hard, a tough, resilient, early-to-rise deputy. For all his cartoon reputation as Mr. Nixon's Svengali, he is by every account fastidious about seeing that all the questions get asked and all the options presented.

For "balance," the magazine quotes Haldeman's critics, but even their words add to an overall admiring picture:

Enemies go with the assignment—"It's part of the job sheet," says another old confrere—but Haldeman has made rather more than his share. Subordinates are afraid of him. Senior officials call his troop of beardless, buttoned-down helpers "the Beaver Patrol." Much of Congress and some of the Republican Party consider him a kind of short-haired Savonarola, contemptuous of them and concerned only for the President. . . .

Together, Nixon and Haldeman make a dazzlingly efficient management team, with work habits as crisp and disciplined as the directors of the best corporations:

Roughly at 9, Mr. Nixon pushes a special button on the side of his five-line telephone and brings Haldeman padding down the 32 paces to the Oval Office, a notebook and a stack of folders bulging under his arm, to preview the day's docket. The President dips into his inside jacket pocket, fishes out a wad of memos he has jotted to himself overnight and has Haldeman tend to them. . . . The President thereafter repairs to his morning appointments and his afternoon "chunks of time"; Haldeman plunges into his chores, dictating memos, rapping orders into a telephone, assembling staff conferences, sitting in on meetings and, lately, riding herd on the sweeping reorganization in progress in the second Nixon Administration.

The timing of the adoring article was unfortunate. In a matter of days the Watergate cover-up began to crumble visibly, and a somewhat different picture of Haldeman emerged.

———

Emmet John Hughes, who worked in the Eisenhower White House, has considered—and discarded—the notion that Nixon was always aware that his words were taped and therefore was deliberately trying "to muddy the record." The tape record, Hughes observed in the *New York Times* magazine of June 9, 1974, "puts forth almost nothing that stands at variance with the political character of Richard Nixon as perceived over a span of 25 years." A final question, then, is: Perceived by whom? For if the tapes reveal the one, the true, the real Nixon, who has been around Washington since 1949—and who has been telling us who he is—then why should this image surprise so many people in the press and generally? How was he able to dissemble for so long?

On one level there was a simple failure of information gathering. Nixon and his men had little trouble creating "gaps" in the public record. Until quite late in the game, as Woodward and Bernstein have said, the White House crew—as inept as it was—still was able to stay ahead of the news business. On another level, apparently, the man had become blurred in the aura of the office of the presidency. While the Imperial Presidency did not begin with Richard Nixon—vide Camelot—he completed the process. And if the shock of recognition when the Nixon transcripts appeared was strongest among newspapers in Middle America—such as the *Chicago Tribune* and the *Kansas City Times*—it may be that their editors got this far in life hoping that national politics are somehow different from

politics in Cook County or Jefferson County. (In all fairness, it should be noted that the corruption of Watergate,
as the University of Chicago law professor Philip Kurland
has pointed out, is of an entirely different nature from
the corruption of party politicians lining their own pockets
from the public till. It is as different as the Dreyfus case
is from the fixing of a traffic ticket.)

Closer to the White House, among working reporters,
other emotions may have been at work. These emotions
included, in unequal parts, fear, uncertainty, an unwillingness to trust the testimony of one's own eyes, and, yes,
a preference for "objectivity." "Reporters leaned over
backward to be as fair and charitable as possible," recalls
one White House correspondent. John Lindsay of *Newsweek* still remembers Daniel P. Moynihan's effusive words
of praise for Richard Nixon at Moynihan's farewell party
a few years ago, an occasion that marked the death of the
Family Assistance Plan as well as Moynihan's departure
for India. "We wanted to believe in a new Nixon,"
Lindsay says. "Moynihan, me and everyone else." Having
been raised so high and bathed so favorably in the media
lights, Richard Nixon could only topple disastrously when
a lifetime's cover-up came apart.

———

What did the press know, and when did it know? As far
as knowledge of Richard Nixon, of his White House, and
of the way his men ran the country, the answer seems to
be: it did not now know very much, what it learned was
learned only belatedly—and precious little of that knowledge gained has been put to use in the continuing coverage of the presidency.

Chapter 11
Myths of Watergate

During an interview with one of his last-ditch loyalists, Rabbi Baruch Korff of Providence, Rhode Island, Richard Nixon declared that if it hadn't been for a vindictive, hostile, liberal press, Watergate would have been no more than a "blip" in history. The interview, granted in May 1974, was not released until July of that year, when the impeachment process dominated attention. Consequently, Nixon's extraordinary reading of events connected with his resignation attracted relatively little comment at the time; so many people were so relieved to see him go that he was allowed the final figleaf of a cover-up.

If nothing else, at least Richard Nixon remained consistent to the end in his public utterances on this narrow point. As early as his televised speech on August 15, 1973, and his news conference of August 22, 1973, Nixon sought to lay his Watergate troubles on the fact that the American public for months had been subjected to a "barrage" of Watergate stories every night for ten or fifteen minutes on the three network news programs. The President made no mention of the testimony of John Dean at the Senate Select Committee hearings, or the work of the special prosecutor, Archibald Cox, or the published memoranda of his Administration— just the evening television newscasts. A few weeks later, in his next news conference, he responded in much the same way to a question about how he intended to restore confidence in his leadership. As he told it, the four months of "leers and sneers of the television commentators" had undermined public confidence in him.

It is difficult to say with certainty whether Richard Nixon really believed that the press "hounded" him from office or whether he was attempting to create a mythology—comforting to him and to his followers—amid the ruins of his presidency. Curiously, there is a mirror image of this mythology on the other side: the notion that the scandals of the Nixon years were courageously exposed by a "vigorous free press" (the system works!). These twin mythologies are self-deluding. They visibly bend the facts and needlessly magnify the "power" of the press. They are rooted in certain serious misreadings of the Nixon years, and how the Watergate scandal was reported.

———

The Watergate coverage divides roughly into three parts: first, the discovery phase, which began on June 17, 1972, the date of the break-in and arrests at Democratic National Committee headquarters; second, the disclosure phase, which began about March 21, 1973, when James McCord, one of the convicted burglars, sent a sealed envelope to Judge John Sirica. The severity of "Maximum John's" provisional sentences had helped McCord rethink the case and get a new lawyer. His letter was unsealed and read in court on March 23, and McCord's accusations of perjury during the Watergate investigation and trial were made public. The third, and final, phase of the story began in mid-May with the start of the Senate Select Committee's televised hearings and ran through the climax of the House Judiciary Committee's impeachment debate—also televised—and the denouement of resignation in the summer of 1974. This might be called the political education phase of the coverage.

HOW "THE SYSTEM" WORKED . .

How "the System" Worked

In the discovery phase, the *Washington Post* was consistently ahead of other newspapers, most notably the *New York Times* and the *Washington Star,* in its reportage (just as, to a lesser extent, *Time* magazine was ahead of its rivals). When this happens—when a news organization appears to "own" a story because of better sources, or more effort or time or money, or plain luck—there is a tendency by its competitors to downgrade the story, if not actually to ignore it. Benjamin Bradlee, the executive editor of the *Post,* vividly recalls the feeling that "we were all alone out there on this story" all during the summer and fall of 1972.[1] When the disclosure phase began, the newspapers, magazines, and television programs overflowed with Watergate news. But that torrent tends to obscure the fact that, in the earlier days, few news organizations had bothered with the story.

Just how "the system" worked can be seen by analyzing the coverage in the first months after the break-in. The press critic Ben H. Bagdikian calculated that, of the 433 Washington-based reporters who could, in theory, have been assigned initially to Watergate, only some 15 actually were, and some of those for only two weeks at a time. The *Washington Post* ombudsman-critic Robert C. Maynard, in a survey of some 500 political columns written between June and November 1972, found that the columnists—the Restons, Krafts, Buckleys, et al.—had produced fewer than two dozen Watergate pieces.

On a somewhat parallel quest, a group of us in the News Study Group in the Department of Political Science, Massachusetts Institute of Technology, analyzed the national television coverage of Watergate during the 1972 presidential election campaign. Beginning shortly after Labor

1972 CAMPAIGN COVERAGE: A C

Day, the traditional start of the main presidential campaign, the News Study Group videotaped all of the regular (Monday through Friday) evening news programs of the three commercial networks. Stenographic transcripts of the accompanying texts also were made, and all pictures and text items related to the election campaign were separated out for classification and coding by computer. In addition, a "scrapbook" was compiled of presidential campaign coverage in such national print outlets as the *New York Times,* the *Washington Post,* and the newsmagazines.[2]

This computer-aided system makes it possible to determine how much time the candidates and their supporters receive on each network's news program, which issues are covered, which speeches are covered, and how the network presents the news, as well as other factors such as use of film and background slides, placement of the story, the nature of the anchorman's and the reporter's commentaries, together with any nonverbal communications accompanying the report.

The 1972 Campaign Coverage: A Computer Analysis

In the specific context of the 1972 campaign, the computer program could isolate, for example, how the Democratic Party headquarters break-in was described on various newscasts: Was it called the "Watergate affair," or the "Watergate case," or the "Watergate caper," or the "Watergate scandal"? And what was the frequency of mention, the emphasis, and the mode of presentation? The computer could also test the complaint of George McGovern, expressed during the campaign, that the networks too literally tried for "balance" by giving him two minutes on

the evening news to denounce, say, the Nixon Administration as one of the most corrupt in history—to be followed by two minutes for denials by one of the Republican surrogates like Ronald Ziegler, Robert Dole, or Clark
MacGregor.

Four members of the News Study Group—Paul Schindler, Jr., Richard Parker, David Olive, and Norman Sandler—
did most of the analysis and were able to sort out some
definite patterns of campaign coverage in general and
specifically about Watergate.

The "ABC Evening News," with Howard K. Smith and
Harry Reasoner, relied mainly on straightforward film reports of speeches, news conferences, and other media
events. ABC's major effort involved weekly film reports
from Columbus, Ohio, described as a "fairly typical American city." In August, at the time of the Republican National Convention, ABC dispatched reporter Jim Kincaid,
a producer, and a film crew to remain in Columbus for
the entire campaign. These reports—about ten—ran from
three to five minutes and closed with "Jim Kincaid in the
ABC city, Columbus, Ohio. . . ."

The "NBC Nightly News" appeared on the tapes and
transcripts as low key, almost bland, in its campaign coverage. The use of a daily calendar backdrop and "here's-
the-kind-of-news-day-it-has-been" introduction by John
Chancellor at the top of the program contributed to a
certain detached feeling. Chancellor at his desk, and the
news items appearing as slides or film on the wall, seemed
to create a physical separation of the news from the newsman; Chancellor often craned around to look at the news
from the viewer's position as if to say, "We are *here* on
your side on this; don't blame us if the news *over there* is

ION TELEVIEWERS GOT . . . CBS B

bad." The correspondents—Catherine Mackin, Richard Valeriani, John Dancy, Douglas Kiker—were more sharply focused.

The News Study Group looked at other campaign-related stories besides Watergate. Among the more notable examples of NBC's efforts in the period recorded was the coverage of Henry Kissinger's news conference of Thursday, October 26, when Kissinger announced that "Peace is at hand." The announcement itself, the worldwide reaction, and its effect on the presidential campaign commanded the first fifteen minutes of the ABC and CBS broadcasts that night. NBC went even further, devoting the entire "Nightly News" to events related to Kissinger's announcement.

The "CBS News with Walter Cronkite" made the most visible departure from the older canons of television news; in the face of cynical dicta about the short attention span of the audience, CBS did longer, more demanding stories touching on the presidential campaign. CBS News also made extensive use of graphics—charts, slides, diagrams, and other techniques normally neglected in this putatively visual medium—and took the unprecedented step of moving anchorman Cronkite from his desk to a standing position in front of a chart illustrating the complexities of the Soviet wheat sale.

These differences between CBS and its rivals in story length and in style were perhaps most evident in the contrasting coverage of the wheat sale. ABC and NBC devoted less time to coverage than did CBS (references to the wheat sale in candidates' speeches and similar circumstances were not counted). Most of the Smith-Reasoner coverage consisted of one six-minute segment reporting on

REAKS THE MOLD . . . THE AGE OI

congressional hearings and quoting farmers who claimed to be cheated in the deal. The Cronkite program, on the other hand, ran about ten stories on the wheat sale, two of them extraordinarily substantial by television standards. On September 27, CBS spent 11 minutes and 11 seconds on the wheat sale. On October 6, it devoted five minutes more to the sale and its possible effects on higher consumer prices. Quoting others, CBS talked of "the great grain robbery." The chromakey (the slide projection in the background) read WHEAT SCANDAL?

The first CBS report began with the announced intention of finding out "who benefited from the sale. . . ." CBS said Agriculture Secretary Earl Butz and other government officials "knew as early as May about the Russian crop failures but withheld news about it." Then Cronkite, proving he was not anchored to his desk, went to a blackboard; pictured on it were two buildings and four men. The figures carried briefcases with their names on them: two people were Agriculture Department officials; two were grain company executives. The figures switched sides. It was strong material, especially in a campaign.

What 45 Million Televiewers Got

On Watergate, the News Study Group's analysis of network performance makes for only slightly less depressing reading than the Bagdikian and Maynard findings. Our replay of the videotape shows that, on Watergate, the 45 to 50 million early evening news watchers received from television news:

1. A fairly steady diet of the headline news from the *Post* and other newspapers. There was little original

OX . . . THE MESSAGE WAS THE M

reporting by any network and almost nothing that could be called investigative reporting.

2.   The usual evenhandedness that has come to mark the style of the evening newscasts. On October 10, for example, when the *Post* broke a major story on the role of Nixon men in alleged political sabotage, NBC's John Chancellor noted the charges at length and then reported: "The Republicans say it's all fiction and we'll have their side in a minute [Break to Commercial]."

3.   A straight, unquestioning serving of "news" that—it is clear, in hindsight—advanced the cover-up. For example, on September 15, the day the indictments of the Watergate Seven were handed down, NBC interviewed the defendants, who spoke of their efforts against an "international Communist conspiracy." Attorney General Richard Kleindienst was shown declaring that Watergate represented "the most thorough FBI investigation ever" with the exception of the John F. Kennedy assassination. NBC also "balanced" comments by Larry O'Brien, the Democratic national chairman, with a statement by his Republican counterpart, Clark MacGregor. In the name of "balance," on another evening NBC devoted extended film coverage to the tortuous facts of a countersuit filed against O'Brien by Maurice Stans, chairman of the Nixon finance committee.

CBS Breaks the Mold

The analysis also shows that there was one major exception to this superstraight, superjudicious coverage: two special reports on Watergate in the "CBS Evening News." In one report, Walter Cronkite spoke of "charges of a high-level campaign of political sabotage and espionage apparently unparalleled in American history. . . ."

ESSAGE

Quantitatively, during the seven-week preelection period beginning on Thursday, September 14, CBS devoted almost twice as much air time to Watergate as either of its competitors. The figures:

CBS   71 minutes, 9 seconds
ABC   42 minutes, 26 seconds
NBC   41 minutes, 21 seconds

More than half of NBC's stories were less than a minute in length; slightly less than half of ABC's were; CBS did minute-or-less items only five times. More than one-third of NBC's Watergate coverage came on two nights, September 15, the date of the grand jury indictments of the Watergate Seven, and October 10, the date of the *Post* story on sabotage. Among the longer ABC stories were an interview with a lawyer who knew alleged political saboteur Donald Segretti (5 minutes, 10 seconds) and man-on-the-street interviews about Watergate in the "ABC city of Columbus, Ohio" (4 minutes, 13 seconds).

One MIT student monitor, Richard Parker, who watched four separate replays of all three networks' coverage, thought that ABC and NBC News "treated Watergate just like another ordinary news story . . . it seemed to be on the air only because the lawsuits, the grand jury, and *Post* stories had to be reported. . . ." CBS, on the other hand, seemed to extend itself with film and arresting graphics.

On September 15, the day of the Watergate indictments, all three network news programs began with long reports. All showed interviews of various principals, but CBS also found and interviewed some of G. Gordon Liddy's associates from his days as a hard-line prosecutor in Dutchess County, New York.

On October 3, when Representative Wright Patman's Banking Committee voted 20 to 15 not to investigate Watergate, CBS allotted 3 minutes and 18 seconds to the story; CBS reporter Lesley Stahl's strong summary said, in part, "the debate itself focused on the questions of infringement of civil liberties and the right of the voters to know the truth before the election. . . ." NBC allotted 34 seconds to the same story, with John Chancellor stating simply that the Democrats "will not get something they wanted badly. . . ."

On October 10, when the story of alleged political sabotage surfaced in the *Washington Post,* NBC's report was twice as long as that of either of its rivals. Balance was evident throughout: the *Post* said a White House aide wrote the "Canuck" letter to damage Senator Edmund Muskie, though the aide denied the report. On CBS, by contrast, not only were the *Post*'s charges repeated, but Daniel Schorr reported further accusations by Democrats. On October 25, when the *Post* named H. R. Haldeman in connection with Watergate, both CBS and NBC gave major attention to the story; ABC dealt with it in 12 seconds.

CBS's "Special Report on Watergate" appeared on October 27. The first 6 minutes and 30 seconds of the Cronkite program were devoted to Vietnam, the President's veto of spending bills, and the Dow Jones prices. Then:

CRONKITE: Watergate, the opening gate for a still unfolding story of political intrigue with ominous implications. We'll be back in a minute with a detailed report on that story.

[One-minute commercial]

CRONKITE (standing in front of dark screen showing buildings identified with tags as Watergate, offices of

CRP—Committee for the Reelection of the President—the
White House): Watergate has escalated into charges of a
high-level campaign of political sabotage and espionage
apparently unparalleled in American history. . . .

CBS returned to Watergate again; beginning Monday,
October 30, in the last week of the campaign, Cronkite
introduced a series of six Special Reports called "The Candidates and the Issues." The Special Reports ranged from
4 minutes, 24 seconds to 8 minutes, 23 seconds in length—
a total of some 41 minutes. The reports allowed the candidates to make their cases on such matters as defense,
welfare, crime, tax reform, and the "pocketbook issues."
The segment on the Watergate "issue" ran about 8 minutes. It had been planned to run 15 minutes—the same
length as the first report. After that first report, White
House aide Charles Colson angrily phoned CBS chairman
William Paley to complain; officially, CBS executives have
since denied that this influenced the follow-up.

———

There are, of course, many things the computer cannot
do. To take an obvious case, totals of broadcast minutes
alone do not convey the quality of the work under study.
Dan Rather, the CBS White House correspondent, offers
a reasonable verdict on broadcast journalism's performance
during the first phase of the Watergate scandal: "CBS
News was putting some stories about Watergate on the
air, more than our broadcast competitors, but pitifully
few. . . ." Rather blames this failure on "the deadly daily
diet of deceit sent us from the White House. Those dishing
this out believed that if the Watergate story could be limited to the *Post,* it could be contained and kept from

spreading. They lied, schemed, threatened and cajoled to prevent network correspondents from getting a handle on the story. And they succeeded."[3]

The Age of Xerox

In late March 1973, when the cover-up plan came apart, both the amount and the solidity of the information available changed. There was no longer any problem about getting a "handle" on the story. Potential defendants—and their lawyers—were going to the prosecutors and talking; some of these lawyers were also talking to reporters, as part of their efforts to obtain favorable deals for their clients. It worked something like this: if the lawyers for John Dean wanted to convey to the prosecutors the "value" of their client to the case, they would make him available for a background interview with a reporter; when a "whiff" of the story appeared, and the prosecutors got the message, they would be more willing to come through with promises of limited immunity or leniency in exchange for the whole story.

In this disclosure phase of the Watergate scandal from March 1973 to the opening of the Senate Select Committee hearings in May 1973, the press was necessarily more the recipient than the active generator of material. The information came out in a torrent: reams of photocopies of White House material that John Dean had taken with him; documents, diaries, logs, and memoranda subpoenaed by the Senate Committee staff. They told the story of the Houston plan, the plumbers' operation, the Ellsberg break-in, the forged cables, enemies' lists, political "hardball" (that is, sabotage and infiltration), the ITT case, the milk funds, the dummy committees, the laundered money. The *New York Times* reprinted almost all the documents verbatim. Television then "brought it all home" to the public, according to Michael Robinson of the Department of Politics, Catholic University.[4] Robinson sampled public opinion in May as the hearings were getting under way, and again in August when they ended. He concluded that "television was the undisputed fount of political information about Watergate." Well before the hearings began, however, the Harris and Gallup polls were showing that a high proportion of the public had *already* made up their minds that Nixon was involved in the Watergate wrongdoing.

Much the same thing happened with the release of the White House tapes on April 30, 1974. The amount of attention on radio and television and in newspapers, magazines, and paperback books was enormous; over 1.5 million copies of the Bantam Book edition alone were sold within seven days of publication, according to the Bantam sales office. But if the testimony of the public opinion polls—and of one's own eyes and ears—is to be believed, then most people had already made up their minds about the "character" of Nixon and his men long before all the press hand-wringing.

Still, the mythology of media power persisted. The columnist Kevin Phillips and the public opinion analyst Albert Sindlinger, in the spring of 1974, laboriously "matched" the press coverage of Nixon and his public ratings.[5] The Phillips-Sindlinger fever chart related the changes in Nixon's job rating to the intensity of press coverage of news that might be judged "favorable" or "unfavorable" to the President. Predictably enough, the Middle East "settlement" drove his ratings up; the release of the first edited presidential conversations sent his ratings plummeting. But their model overlooked the fact that

Nixon's ratings dropped below 50 percent as early as April 1973 and that the overall downward slope never changed direction significantly despite the week-to-week ups and downs.

The Message Was the Message

The record of the Watergate coverage discloses no hounding of the President. Quite the contrary. The press did not speak as a chorus with one voice. The President had his own defenders; equally important, his noncampaign's noncommunications in 1972 initially came across louder than the message of Watergate. Ultimately, it was not the "power" of the press but the substance of the evidence— in the Senate documents, in the House Committee's 39 volumes of information, and in the President's own behavior—that was decisive. The message, not the medium, was the message. Eventually, some of the President's conservative supporters saw that; on the day of the resignation, the *Dallas News* noted in an editorial that the Nixon Administration had been subjected to "many vicious, unfair and reprehensible attacks." But, the paper added, the Nixon Administration was "brought down by the failings of Richard M. Nixon himself."

Perhaps the sharpest blow to the mythmaking that followed Richard Nixon's downfall came, appropriately, from "public opinion." Right after the resignation, there was a considerable amount of earnest speculation about a "backlash" developing against the press for its presumed role in bringing down the President. It was perhaps natural for some of the press to cast themselves as central figures on the stage of history; but the scenario proved faulty. First of all, the idea of backlash itself was somewhat tainted. The most notorious media use of the word

came in the mid-1960s with the supposed "white backlash" to civil rights gains. But when the Harvard social
scientist J. Michael Ross investigated the "backlash," he
found literally no basis for it: no one had adequately measured white attitudes toward black social and economic
progress in the years *before* the civil rights movement.[6]
Thus, there was no real way of knowing if the percentage
of white opposition to further black "progress" was higher—a backlash—or lower than, or the same as, before the
movement. The same kind of baseline approach can help
put "press backlash" stories in perspective. In general,
about one-third to one-fourth of the people in the public
opinion samplings taken over the last decade (when this
question became fashionable) have been highly critical of
the press for its alleged bias. There is no firm evidence that
this group has changed in size significantly during the
years of the Watergate coverage. Like most institutions in
American society, the press shared in the general decline
in public confidence registered in the Louis Harris polls
from the mid-1960s on. Typically, the majority of the
public tends to treat the press—quite properly, in my opinion—as just one more of the goods and services of society;
this sensible majority makes judgments mainly on a case-
by-case basis. These nonprofessionals do not continually
take the press's pulse and check its temperature. Immediately after the evidence of Watergate scandal came spill-
ing out in the spring of 1973, the press's job ratings went
up; later, a certain public "weariness with Watergate" set
in. Rabbi Korff, the Nixon loyalist and a mythmaker past
the bitter end, announced he would lead a crusade against
the "big media." He found few followers and quickly
passed from public sight. The sensible majority—sharing
neither the Rabbi's devil theories nor the press's

professional hypochondria with its own well-being—had moved on to other matters of immediate concern, such as food prices and mortgage money.

———

Although the press did not occupy center stage in the Nixon drama, it was not without influence. But its influence was limited. The press cannot, like grand juries and officers of the law, subpoena evidence or compel testimony. It has no legal powers. But it has freedom. One of the fascinating "what ifs" of the Watergate scandal is: What if one or two or all three of the network news organizations had behaved like the *Washington Post?* What if the voters had fully realized the extent of corruption and cover-up before election day in November 1972? Frank Mankiewicz, a leading strategist in the McGovern campaign, said that if all of Watergate had spilled out, the margin of the Nixon victory might have been smaller, but nothing would have prevented President Nixon's reelection. Similarly, Theodore White said that Watergate would have had "the weight of a feather" in the campaign. They may be right; but the press's chief job in a campaign is not to elect, or to defeat; it is to make sure that sufficient information, in understandable form, is available to the voters, who do the electing. That is where real press "power" lies. Each news organization ought to ask itself if in 1972 this power was exercised, and how well. The record deflates the myth.

Chapter 12
Media Blitz!

The creative talent from the advertising agency of Lois Holland Callaway, Inc., has, in the past, done television commercials for New York Senator Jacob Javits's Republican campaign in 1962, for Robert F. Kennedy's Democratic campaign for Senator from New York in 1964, for Republican-turned-Independent John V. Lindsay's re-election campaign in the 1969 mayoralty race in New York City, and for the 1970 campaign of Senator Hugh Scott of Pennsylvania. In each of these races, the agency's "entry" won the election—and, according to founding partner Jim Callaway, the political commericals designed by the agency were significant factors in the victories. The Javits commercials, for example, indirectly addressed themselves to the sensitive issue of the Senator's role as a liberal "in the more conservative party." In a 60-second commercial, filmed in cinema verité style, Javits was shown discussing, with a street crowd, "Why I am a Republican. . . ." Similarly, the Kennedy commericals confronted the potentially damaging "carpetbagger issue"—Kennedy had never lived in New York State, except for a brief time when he was a child—with the line "Let's Put Robert Kennedy to Work for New York." The Lindsay commercials confronted still another negative issue—the known animosity of great numbers of New Yorkers to him because of many of his "mistakes" during his first term (the subway strike, the great Queens snow removal fiasco, among others).[1] According to Callaway, Tony Isadore of the Lois Holland Callaway agency created a brilliant commercial in which Lindsay frankly admitted some of his mistakes and also pointed out some of his triumphs. The commercial ended with the Isadore line "It's the second-toughest job in America."

Given this kind of track record in political campaigns, Callaway naturally engages our attention when he declares, "Let's Cut Out the Baloney about Political Advertising." "I am bored to distraction with all the foolishness being written and spoken about political advertising," Callaway wrote in *Politeia*, the quarterly journal of the American Association of Political Consultants. "I'm tired of press 'exposés' of media manipulators who package candidates as if they were bars of soap. They've got it backwards—we *can* sell candidates, it's almost impossible to sell soap."[2]

This is a fresh variation on an old theme. Most advertising people claim that they can sell soap and candidates; the adman Paul Stevens entitled his book on television commercials *I Can Sell You Anything*. Billions of dollars are spent each year on television and newspaper advertising in order to sell soap—and beer, deodorants, cigarettes, and other products that are, at most, only marginally different. Millions of dollars more are spent during political campaigns to sell candidates; in the 1968 presidential election campaign, an estimated $20 million was spent for television on behalf of Richard Nixon. In addition, considerable energy was exerted by the Nixon campaign advisers to create an image of candidate Nixon that would come across well in living rooms. The zenith of this effort—or nadir, depending on your point of view—was reached on election eve, 1968; Nixon appeared on a

A MODEST EXPERIMENT . . . THE R

nationally televised "telethon" to answer questions
ostensibly phoned in by the voters. Joe McGinniss, in
his account of the Nixon election effort, *The Selling of
the President*, described how Frank Shakespeare (formerly of CBS), Paul Keyes (once executive producer of
the "Laugh-in Show"), and Roger Ailes (an alumnus of
the "Merv Griffin Show") carefully staged-managed the
telethon details right down to the way telephoned questions would be "properly worded" on the air in order to
conform to the questions Mr. Nixon wanted to answer.
As McGinniss tells it, just before air time the studio
received an extra blast of cold air: "I can't do that sin-
cerity bit with the camera if he's sweating," the director
says. As the program goes on the air, Roger Ailes
observes, "This is the beginning of a whole new concept.
This is it. This is the way they'll be elected forevermore.
The next guys up will have to be performers."

The dust jacket of the McGinniss book repeats this
theme: on it is a cigarette package with a picture of
Richard Nixon serving as the "label."

A Modest Experiment

Jim Callaway may have been making a self-deprecating
little joke when he suggested that advertisers can't sell
soap. He is right, however, about all the foolishness that
has been written and spoken about political advertising.
Fortunately, a check of sorts is possible. The Congress
of the United States several years ago made possible an
interesting experiment that seemed to serve, though
quite unintentionally, as a test of the claims for advertising, especially television advertising. The experiment
involves cigarettes, rather than soap; nevertheless, it helps

cut down on a lot of the exaggerated claims made in recent years.

In 1964, the United States Surgeon General determined that cigarette smoking was implicated in lung cancer and other diseases. After years of agitation by health groups and consumer advocates, Congress voted to prohibit all advertising for cigarettes on radio and television beginning on January 2, 1971.[3] Congress's action was clearly discriminatory against broadcasting, since magazines, newspapers, and other print outlets were under no similar prohibition. Print advertising and television advertising were treated differently for the obvious constitutional reason that the federal government has no direct control over print; broadcasting, while also enjoying First Amendment protection, is still subject to federal licensing and regulation. But Congress would probably have found a way around the Constitution if it had thought the objective of stopping cigarette advertising *completely* was important enough. It did not. Cigarette ads on television were singled out from all other advertising mainly because just about everyone concerned in the controversy, the smoking forces as well as the antismoking forces, accepted the same proposition: since television exerts such a powerful influence on behavior—in particular, on the behavior of the "impressionable" young—it has to be treated as qualitatively different from all other media. (It was much the same reasoning about the "power" of television that led Congress to pass the 1972 federal campaign law limiting broadcast expenditures for candidates.)

And so on January 2, 1971 (Congress, in a last act of compassion, permitted the cigarette advertisers to make, in the words of the *Wall Street Journal*, "one final

KENNEDY-NIXON DEBATES . . .

onslaught" on viewers during the New Year's Day football bowl games), two decades of television advertising ended. The Marlboro cowhand lit up his final smoke for the last video roundup, the last beautiful couple romped through the springtime fresh woods in the Salem commerical for the last time, the animated Doral cigarettes strutted through their last dance, and the Virginia Slims baby, who had come a long way, could go no further on television.

The Television Bureau of Advertising estimated that some $157 million worth of cigarette advertising business was lost to the networks in 1971, the first year of the ban. Another $59 million in radio advertising was also lost. The $216-plus million had paid for thousands of minutes of cigarette commercials, which had been seen or heard at one time or another by just about every one of the 150 million Americans over six years old with access to a radio or television set. Interestingly, however, the television industry's loss of revenue was *not* matched by a similar downturn in the fortunes of the cigarette industry. In 1971, in fact, the consumption of cigarettes in the United States *increased* by 2.33 percent. Even if the growth in population is taken into account, there was a per capita increase in cigarette smoking. Again, in 1972, cigarette consumption increased, this time by 3.1 percent; both increases occurred despite the fact that the price of a package of cigarettes had increased in 1971 and 1972.

Several explanations have been put forward by the experts for this seemingly strange state of affairs—when they can be persuaded to discuss the matter, for no great roll of drums has accompanied the release of the figures. The

average citizen's first reaction might be to conclude that
advertising had little influence on smoking behavior. Period. But, it might be argued, at the same time that the cigarette commercials for Marlboro and Salem went off the
air, the antismoking commericals of the American Cancer
Society and the American Heart Association *also* went off
the air. In this view, the power of television advertising
to influence behavior appears undimmed: the two persuasive forces had neutralized each other. As might be expected, this view is shared by television sales divisions and
by the advertising industry.

A second explanation runs something like this: Smoking per se is such an attractive habit—and so ingrained
once begun—that the mere absence of reinforcing advertising is not important. People become physically addict-
ed to the chemical ingredients in the tobacco itself and
not to any of the psychological "aura" of smoking created by advertising (by, for example, the usual message
that says a particular brand of cigarettes makes you
socially desirable). In the case of cigarettes, the argument
goes, the real purpose of a good part of the advertising
was not to persuade people to take up the habit but was
to get the addicts to move from one brand name to another because it delivers some alleged marginal bonus,
such as less tar or more "coolness" (and you *look* cool
smoking its new long shape). This has been the view of
many tobacco company people. Television, a Tobacco
Institute official told me, may do nothing to expand the
mature—that is, regular—smokers' market. Rather, its
selling ability lies in introducing new brands. The tobacco companies' public behavior after the ban has reflected
this line of reasoning; while much of the cigarette

N "NEW POLITICS" . . . "SELECTIV

advertising budget was shifted in part to other, "less effective" media, such as magazines, billboards, and newspapers, the companies simply spent 28 percent *less* for advertising in 1971. "During this period of sharply lower spending and reduced exposure to cigarette ads," the Tobacco Institute noted blandly in its 1971 annual report, "domestic consumption rose. . . ."

Probably each of these arguments helps explain to some degree the increase in cigarette smoking over the last few years. But at least one other explanation also seems possible: it may be true that advertising "works"—that it moves goods and services—but it may also be true that no one knows with any degree of confidence why and when and how a television message is more or less effective. "Looking at all the sales and advertising data over the last ten years," the Tobacco Institute official concludes, "I can't justify a contention that (a) TV was effective in 'unselling' smoking or (b) that it was effective in selling smoking."

———

If the makers of cigarettes, after spending hundreds of millions of dollars each year on advertising, are still uncertain of its effects, then how much more problematic are the effects of messages when advertising moves into the area of "selling" public policy issues or political candidates? How predictable can the results be when advertising moves beyond the relatively controlled situation of a commercial message—where the time of day, the kind of audience, the tone and style of the delivery can all be carefully selected—to the relatively unstructured,

LEVISION . . . CONFESSIONS OF A

freewheeling situation of a congressional hearing on Watergate, a political debate, or a "Meet the Press" interview?

The Rise of Living Room Politics

Politics, as the adman Rosser Reeves once observed, has much in common with advertising—"it is a feedback business, with success to those who know what the public wants to hear." The critic Martin Mayer also concluded that the modern mass-market candidate, like the modern mass-market product, must try to please as many people as possible. "Because the tube brought the candidate into the voter's home," Mayer has written, "inoffensiveness acquired a high premium. . . ." Insults, diatribe, and invective—all the color that had made politics interesting and human for centuries—did not go over well on television, and were dropped from the mass candidates' repertoire. Like commercial products and like television personalities themselves, the rough edges of the product had to be smoothed, because the sale was taking place in the intimacy of the living room.

Advertising is not new to politics. Newspapers, billboards, and radio have all long been used in political campaigns; but the explosive growth of television set ownership beginning in the 1950s provided a new way to reach voters. In the past, the prospective voter had to go out of the house to make some personal connection with the candidate. Now the candidate—or, more precisely, an image of the candidate—could come into the prospective voter's home. This could be done for a price in a paid commercial appearance, or free on news or public affairs programs. The candidate could engage the voter in the "intimacy" of the living room. It was usually expensive;

N EX-IMAGE MAKER . . . THE OTTI

in New York, a candidate for governor might have to spend some $4.5 million, or 50 cents a household, to get his television message into each of the 8 to 9 million living rooms of likely voters in the state.[4] But it seemed absolutely necessary.

The economics of living room politics appeared to transform electoral campaigns. Candidates, it seemed, had to have huge financial resources; they also had to have image makers—experts in creating commercials, buying time, and stage-managing campaign events. As early as 1952, Rosser Reeves and Robert Montogmery, the actor turned television producer, were coaching Dwight D. Eisenhower on his television appearances. Herbert Alexander, director of the Citizens Research Foundation and a knowledgeable observer of campaigning expenditures, offered this concise account of broadcasting's effects on politics in the years between 1952 and 1960:

With the advent of television, campaign itineraries and speeches were timed for prime viewing hours to get maximum audiences. National nominating conventions are scheduled with a view to providing maximum exposure to the American people while putting the party in the best possible light. Presidential candidates now seem to be chosen in the open—before the eyes of the cameras and the public—rather than in smoke-filled rooms. Television makes it possible for candidates to reach the farthest corners of a constituency, and it makes candidates more familiar to the electorate. Candidates are sometimes chosen because they have appealing personalities, smiling families, and good television presence. Sometimes issues are left undefined and positions unclarified as candidates project their personalities and toss irrelevancies into campaigns to attract attention. When candidates are nominated and campaign on personal factors, the parties tend to be downgraded and become less important. The candidate is not necessarily a party personage, but a popular

EFFECT . . . THE OLD POLITICS . .

personality in his own right. Some believe that a leader
with access to radio and television facilities and a forum
like the White House or a governor's mansion has little
need for the party organization and machinery to achieve
his electoral success.[5]

Television and the image specialists seemed about to
bury the political party system and traditional political
campaigns. By the 1960s, a "new politics" was being
heralded. The weighty (four volumes, 3,959 pages) *History of American Presidential Elections 1789-1968,* edited
by Professor Arthur M. Schlesinger, Jr., and F. L. Israel,
described how the political parties progressively lost their
capacity to mobilize voters while the mass media grew in
power. "Television, the public opinion poll and the computer began to devastate the traditional political structure," Schlesinger wrote in his introduction; politicians
now faced the electorate "eyeball to eyeball" by courtesy of the living room television set.

The Kennedy-Nixon Debates
The 1960 campaign of John F. Kennedy seemed to be the
apotheosis of the "new politics." The term loosely covered a number of elements; on one level, technology and
social science research were mobilized in campaigning.
Scientific polling techniques were used to gauge strategy—
for example, the best way to meet the "Catholic issue."[6]
Computers helped to build a simulated model of the electorate and to test the strategy, and television was used to
acquaint voters with the candidate. Candidate Kennedy
was youthful looking, vigorous, attractive, and fast on his
feet; in a word, he was telegenic. Less well known than
his experienced opponent Richard Nixon, Kennedy decided on an election strategy that would increase his
"recognition factor" through a series of televised debates.

THE "NEWSWORTHY" CAMPAIGN

Nixon had wanted one "sudden death" debate; Kennedy's advisers wanted a debate "every night" if possible. In 1960, almost eight out of every ten households owned a television set; the debates were watched in an estimated 40 million homes. Elmo Roper, the public polltaker, reported that 57 percent of presidential voters, or about 38 million people, said later that the debates had influenced their votes; an additional 6 percent, or 4 million voters, said the debates actually decided their voting. Some 3 million of these "TV votes" went to Kennedy, and 1 million to Nixon. Kennedy's margin of victory in the 1960 election was, it will be recalled, 110,000 votes. A year later, presidential science adviser Jerome Wiesner brought Vladimir Zworykin, the inventor of the vacuum tube, around to the White House. As Wiesner recalls it, he told Kennedy, "Thanks to this man, you're President." Four years later, writing in the *Saturday Evening Post*, Nixon himself offered his own postmortem, seemingly confirming the general opinion that he had lost the debate, and the the election, because of his "untelegenic" appearance:

I suppose I should have anticipated that I might look worn and washed out on camera. Laid up for two weeks with a serious knee infection, I had left the hospital four or five days before my doctor wanted me to and embarked on two weeks of intensive campaigning, propstopping across the country, making six and eight speeches a day. Two days before the debate, I got a bad case of flu and was still running a temperature during the program. I had lost so much weight that my shirt collar hung loosely on my neck and my suit looked baggy. But although I was physically exhausted, I didn't feel tired. I was so intent on the battle that I never stopped to think about how I looked. I have always detested make-up. I didn't like the feel of it or the idea of wearing it. All I did before the program was to shave as closely as I could and apply some powder with a beard stick. If I had a

HAT GETS THROUGH?

make-up man—as my opponent quite properly did—he could have predicted the result: the powder failed to hide my beard but made my skin look even paler.

All these accounts, however, overlooked a key point: Richard Nixon went into the debates because the polls showed that he was running *behind* Kennedy—as much as 10 percentage points behind in one private poll.

The Oracle of Toronto

No matter. The age of "media politics" was legitimized with the debates. Image had taken a place next to substance in politics; everyone talked about the Kennedy style. In time a major prophet arose to reveal the philosophy of the new age. He was Professor Marshall McLuhan, one of the major celebrities of the 1960s. Professor McLuhan's speculations covered a truly extraordinary range of human activities. Among his best-known views was the notion that the development of new electronic forms for the transmission of experience, such as television, wholly transforms that experience; "the medium is the message," as McLuhan said in his Delphic style. There were corollaries of this new "law." McLuhan also proposed that the print medium was "hot"—that is, crammed with information and facts. On the other hand, the television medium was "cool" and undefined. As far as American electoral politics was concerned, the elevation of McLuhan began in mid-October 1960, when Professor McLuhan, after watching the televised Nixon-Kennedy debates, predicted in a newspaper interview that the "cool" John Kennedy would win the election over the "hot" Richard Nixon. On television, McLuhan said, it was more important to appear as a "cool, nonchalant, low-definition" political candidate than as a "hot, forceful, high-definition" candidate. McLuhan's reputation as a modern communications oracle was further enhanced when he later predicted—after watching a more informal, apparently wise Nixon in relaxed conversation on the "Jack Paar Show"—that Nixon would win the presidency the next time around. It was only a matter of time before McLuhan had been expropriated by the advertising business. One of his early disciples, Howard Gossage, a San Francisco advertising executive, declared in an interview that McLuhan was "an Archimedes who has given our industry the levers to move the world. . . ."

The media levers were pulled mightily in the 1968 presidential campaign of Richard Nixon. If Nixon and his campaign advisers didn't actually move the world, they were, by offering the "New" Nixon, able to win the White House. As the reporter Joe McGinniss and other commentators told it, a band of Madison Avenue image makers took Richard Nixon in hand and, thanks to the "adroit manipulation and use of television," waged a consummately successful political campaign. The one-man-on-camera technique—the talking head of the 1950s—was obsolete. Harry Treleavan, director of advertising for the Nixon effort, explained that issues needn't be involved in the campaign. Most national issues are so complex and hard to understand that they intimidate or bore average citizens, according to Treleavan; to win, the candidate has to convince the voters that he really wants to be elected and is working hard at it—people sympathize with hard work and are flattered by the attention.

The New "New Politics"

The term "new politics" was given a new and sour definition: conduct polls to find out the qualities people

want in a President and how people see the candidate in
relation to that; then overcome the gap through controlled television. One form of controlled television was
the telethon, stage-managed sessions in which viewers telephone in questions to the candidate for an hour or two or
more. The other, more frequently used form was the 30-
second or 60-second commercial "spot" flashing a single
slogan, an impression, an "image." The spots designed by
Doyle Dane Bernbach for the Lyndon Johnson campaign
in 1964 were considered perhaps the most effective of
the form; one series implied that the election of Senator
Barry Goldwater, the Republican candidate, would bring
nuclear war closer. A spot showed a little girl picking
daisies, moving across an open field . . . a mushroom cloud
fills the air . . . LBJ's voice says, "These are the stakes
. . . to make a world in which all of God's children can
live . . . or to go into the dark. We must either love each
other . . . or we must die." DDB's pride in its handiwork
had evaporated in a few years: the Johnson who had
escalated the Vietnam War, some of the DDB people
came to believe, was not the Johnson they had sought
to portray.

There were others still willing to perform. In the 1968
campaign, according to John E. O'Toole, president of
Foote, Cone and Belding Communications, Inc., some 70
percent of television advertising was in the form of spots.
O'Toole, like DDB, was so upset by the "trickery" of the
spot message that he wouldn't let his own agency take
political accounts. The format of the television spot particularly upset him. "Ten-second, thirty-second, even
sixty-second lengths," O'Toole wrote in the *Columbia
Journalism Review* in 1972, "are inadequate and inappropriate for presenting a candidate to the voter. These

lengths defy a discussion of issues and encourage the shallowest kind of imagery, the shoddiest kind of logic, and the most reprehensible mudslinging."

Again, however, upon closer examination the use of controlled television proved to be somewhat less important than billed. It is doubtful that there was anything Lyndon Johnson—or Barry Goldwater, for that matter—could have done in the course of the campaign in 1964 that would have decisively affected the outcome. Johnson was well ahead in the polls from the start, and his lead hardly wavered; the media campaign made little net difference. In 1968, however, the "new politics" did make a difference—though not in the manner intended. In the presidential election, the apostles of the modern Archimedes had to explain just what the Nixon media campaign achieved. If the Nixon forces were so shrewd in their use of the media, then how can we account for the fact that (1) their candidate started with a 15-point lead in the polls over Hubert Humphrey in August and (2) by the first week in November—after spending perhaps as much as $20 million on television and radio advertising—Nixon was barely one point ahead?[7] The political strategist Joseph Napolitan later was to argue that the Nixon rollback was due largely to the television campaign of Hubert Humphrey that Napolitan's efforts had created. Napolitan explained all of this in his 1972 book *The Election Game and How to Win It*, which concluded with a chapter entitled "How to Beat Richard Nixon in 1972." Since 1972, Napolitan has been advising political clients outside the United States.

"Selective" Television

None of these doubts about the Nixon "media blitz" slowed the television bandwagon appreciably. However,

campaign advisers attempted to find more selective uses
of television advertising and promotion. Television campaigns, for one thing, seemed to be more effective when
used in primary races rather than in general elections.
This was so because television, demonstrably, could increase the recognition of a relative unknown. In 1970,
Howard Metzenbaum, a wealthy businessman with no
political experience or public image, challenged John
Glenn, the first American astronaut to orbit the earth,
in the Ohio Democratic primary for a U.S. Senate seat.
Metzenbaum started with a 15 percent recognition to
Glenn's 99 percent. Metzenbaum made 14 TV spots,
saturating Ohio for four months before the primary and
won by 14,000 votes; Glenn concluded: "You can buy an
election." In the Texas Democratic primary for U.S.
Senate that same year, the conservative millionaire Lloyd
Bentsen eliminated the incumbent liberal Ralph Yarborough with an intensive spot campaign. In the New
York Democratic primary for U.S. Senate, Representative Richard Ottinger had served three terms in House
but was known to less than one-third of all New York
Democrats four months before primary. Ottinger spent
over $600,000 on television ads and beat out, among
others, the former John Kennedy aide Theodore Sor-
ensen (who was high on political credentials but low on
money). The campaign, designed by David Garth, featured the slogan "Ottinger Delivers."

Television also seemed to be the single most effective
means of reaching most voters in the megastates; how
else could the political message be delivered to the 12
million potential voters of New York or the 11 million
registered voters of California? In the California governor's race in 1970, the former actor Ronald Reagan

spent $1 million for television time and defeated the un-telegenic—and broke—Democratic candidate Jesse Unruh. Marquis Childs wrote in his column, "Here in the Golden West you don't run for office, you pose for office. Image is all important and television is supreme."[8]

Primaries aren't elections, and California isn't the United States. Before the congressional and governors' races in 1970, most of the press and the candidates were still dazzled by media politics. "It is fair to say that the medium *is* much of the message in this fall's elections," *Newsweek* magazine said in its national affairs section. "The selling of the candidates is in many respects a more compelling story than their politics." The magazine then proceeded to describe the "selling of the candidates" rather than the politics of the campaign.

The Confessions of an ex-Image Maker

The results of the 1970 elections had an immediately sobering effect. Many of the candidates who had em-ployed high-priced image makers were beaten. In an elec-tion postmortem, entitled "Value for Money?" *The Econ-omist* of London concluded, "After all the fuss and flurry of professional managers, image makers and media direc-tors, television was not the all-powerful force that it was trumped up to be. Out of the 38 candidates under the guidance of media experts, only 17 won their elections."[9]

It ought to be pointed out that, generally, only those candidates in trouble tended to hire image makers in the first place. In Texas, Lloyd Bentsen spent $900,000 in his media campaign. His opponent Ralph Yarborough had only $150,000 available for a two-week effort. Yar-borough was a liberal in an increasingly illiberal state. Bentsen was younger and more conservative. One of the image makers hired to help Yarborough was a New York adman named Barry Nova who had worked for Hubert Humphrey in 1968 and had formed his own firm, Campaign Planners, in 1970. Campaign Planners had Yarborough and John Glenn for clients. Of Yarborough, Nova later observed,

In past elections, Ralph Yarborough had campaigned in a station wagon at County Court Houses. The record player in the back seat blared out "The Yellow Rose of Texas," and Ralph would talk about bringing the jam jar down to the lower shelf so the little people could get a taste.

He won that way.

All of a sudden, in 1970, his friends went out and hired "image-makers." I was one of them. Yarborough never knew or comprehended what we did. Here were these two guys from New York with a lot of hair telling him how to communicate. He was offended and uncomfortable. One day we presented a group of television commercial story boards. He indicated he liked them, and added, "They seem like awfully big brochures. How are we going to mail them?"

He lost that way. With our help. . . .

Of John Glenn, Nova said,

He was a great astronaut and a valid national hero. He was also shallow of thought; pedantic in speech; and an egocentric. To this day, I don't know what he stands for; neither do the people of Ohio.

At the beginning Glenn just couldn't lose. Who the hell was Metzenbaum, anyway? Prognosticators were predicting a primary win with between 60% and 70% of the vote. However, they failed to take into consideration a number of factors: a bad staff, dedicated solely to headquarters infighting to see who would be the one to walk Glenn down the aisle of the United States Senate chamber; no appreciable money (John rose above that type of nitty-gritty necessity); a total disregard for media; and a rampant overconfidence.

We finally convinced Glenn to do a Q & A shoot so he could have some media presence during the last few weeks. But he didn't answer questions very well. In our pollution spot, a lady asked what he was going to do about it; even with our talent for editing, the 30-second commercial went something like this:

Glenn (on camera): "That's a very important question. I'm glad you asked it. Pollution blows and flows across state lines. [He wrote that line himself and absolutely adored it.] We have to stop it now. Strong laws against polluters would help. It's really an important issue. I'm glad you asked that question. I hope I've answered it well."

Super (over action) [words superimposed over picture]: "Once in a great while a man like John Glenn comes along."[10]

The Ottinger Effect

Nova was out of business in early 1972. Other heavier-weight creative figures went down as well. Harry Treleavan, the advertising man in the Nixon 1968 campaign, had five clients in the 1970 races; four lost. The media campaign of Representative Ottinger was particularly instructive. David Garth's television blitz for Ottinger in the Democratic primary race depicted a vigorous, attractive, youthful candidate campaigning in shirt sleeves. In the general election, however, Democratic candidate Ottinger faced Republican incumbent Charles Goodell and Conservative candidate James Buckley in four live television debates. Each time, Ottinger failed to deliver, scoring a poor third to the others. The live debates revealed him to be somewhat slow and unsure of himself—pleasant, no doubt, but certainly not the decisive figure in his commerical spots. This dissonance between the image and the reality doomed his race, though winning him a footnote of sorts in the history of campaigns:

the impression created by the gap between the image maker's *image* of the candidate and the actual candidate has come to be known as "The Ottinger Effect."

Ottinger was only one of a dozen inflated candidates who failed. The overall record of the image makers in the 1970 elections was so dismal that a postelection conference called at the University of Maryland to celebrate the achievements of the "new politics" almost turned into a funeral service.[11]   Professor Ithiel Pool of MIT and Frederick Papert of the Papert, Koenig and Lois advertising agency, among other conferees, suggested that the alleged manipulative powers of the camera resided more in the self-promoting spiels of the image makers than in any solid evidence. In a way, media politics was the victim of self-inflicted wounds. With each new campaign, the image makers encountered increasingly skeptical voters; the audience had become familiar, nightly, with the techniques of television advertising. Barry Nova ended his image-making career with the observation that "Either the candidates did not understand the advertising men, or the advertising men did not understand the candidates, or the public understood both all too well."

———

The contemporary consumer of the media has received enough instruction to realize that the political adman's slogans are often interchangeable—or meaningless. The "artful" staging of the commercials is often transparent. The first ten times a television spot featured a Kennedy-esque "action" candidate, with shirt collar open and shirt sleeves rolled up, striding down a city sidewalk or peering at a suburban wetland, it was probably quite effective in creating a good impression ("He made the streets safe," "He will protect the environment"). But when that same basic idea is borrowed and constantly recycled—and when the fat, fiftyish, tongue-tied candidate for presiding supervisor of the town of North Hempstead is shown in the same situation—very few voters are likely to be influenced.

The Old Politics

By the time of the national elections in 1972, a measure of balance had been restored to discussions of image candidates. The extravagant claims for media politics were being muted. Once again, campaign managers were practicing the old politics of registration of voters, precinct organization, identification of undecideds, and getting out the vote on election day. There were, of course, candidates who still put their money and energy into a media blitz: Arkansas Representative Wilbur Mills in the New Hampshire Democratic presidential primary, John Lindsay in the Florida Democratic presidential primary, and Senator Henry Jackson in the Wisconsin Democratic presidential primary were among the most prominent users of television in 1972. Mills spent $80,000 and got 4 percent of the vote (compared to Senator Edmund Muskie's 47 percent for $65,000); Lindsay spent $170,000 for 7 percent (compared to Governor George Wallace's 42 percent for $75,000). The losers' expenditures were not totally wasted. For example, Mills was a major power in Washington but was unknown in New Hampshire; his heavy advertising campaign did increase his recognition factor. Student members of the News Study Group at MIT confirmed this by asking voters in two comparable small towns—one in New Hampshire where Mills's television ads had appeared, and one in New York State, where he was not running—who Wilbur Mills was. Nine out of ten of the New Yorkers didn't know; seven out of ten of the New Hampshire voters did. But the failure of the various media blitz candidates in the 1972 primaries underlined the commonsense point that the "experts" should have realized all along: political advertising is only one element in a campaign.

Advertising is a very trendy business. After the debacle of the 1972 primaries, few advertising people could be found who would say a good word *for* political commercials. Roger Ailes, who had proclaimed the new era of the controlled television performer on election eve, 1968, now allowed that a heavy campaign of TV spots was "not the only answer." The voters of the 1970s, the new wisdom held, were relying increasingly on television news and—hold on—print to help make up their minds about candidates. The TV commercial had lost credibility. Uncontrolled television was the way to use the medium. Political consultants now advised their clients to get on the evening television news—to make news, not commercials. Candidates had to stage *media events,* that is, campaign stops and meetings that serve the television news programs' desire for good film and "visuals." The content of the "visuals" was not as important as the timing; events had to be staged early enough in the day so that the film or videotape could be processed and brought back to the studio in time to make the newscast.

The "Newsworthy" Campaign

Candidates also were told to make themselves available for interviews and walk-on appearances in the uncontrolled conditions of live television. Walter De Vries, a

University of Michigan political scientist (now at Duke University) and an adviser to Republican candidates, was one of the apostles of the "newsworthy" campaign; he argued that the news audience was most likely to be voters. In 1972, De Vries advised Nixon's staff that Nixon would err if he used very much television advertising in the campaign. "You can't make him any better known," said Professor De Vries, "and you sure aren't going to make him loved. Those are the only things paid television is good for." As it happened, the Committee to Reelect the President (CRP) spent $8 million—out of the $14 million total it had initially allotted for the 1972 campaign—for television advertising and time. The Nixon strategy emphasized the use of surrogates—Republican officials, Cabinet officers, the Nixon faimly—to stage the news events that would make the news programs.

On the other side, the Democratic ticket of George Mc-Govern and Sargent Shriver worked mightily to make news. McGovern's days often stretched through 16 hours of jet-assisted visits to three different media markets, moving from the East Coast to the West Coast to keep the time zone working in the candidate's interest.

Thomas Collins of *Newsday*, the Long Island newspaper, observantly describes a typical campaign day during 1972 when George McGovern went in search of free television exposure:

The scene was Dubrow's cafeteria in the heart of Manhattan's garment center, one of Sen. George McGovern's first media stops in his campaign for the state's 278 delegates to be elected in the June 20 primary.

To the untutored eye, it wasn't much of a rally. There were only about 500 in the crowd, and many of them were standing with arms folded when the candidate might reasonably have expected applause. But then the rally really wasn't aimed at the live audience. It was designed for the television cameras, and the prospect of picking up a couple of million viewers on that evening's news shows.

McGovern went through all the accepted motions: a press conference before about 80 newsmen and seven TV cameras, a speech on 38th Street and Seventh Avenue, and a chicken liver sandwich that he ate while the cameras recorded the moment for history. . . .

It is all a kind of ritualistic dance that neither partner ever grows tired of performing. You wonder what would happen if McGovern went out on 38th Street and found everyone except a few sightseers had gone home.

Of course, it would never happen, and the candidates know that. So the media is the focal point of the campaigns. You schedule a garment center stop, then tour a Harlem hospital, make a speech in front of Brooklyn Borough Hall, a couple of quick appearances in Syracuse, Albany and Buffalo, and you've done the state, or rather the press has done the state for you.

No candidate is better attuned to the media and its needs than McGovern, and his staff is quite candid about the use of it. Ask a top aide whether the Dubrow thing really was a circus, and he will admit it was. "You schedule stuff early enough for the six o'clock news and you try to get the best photographic possibilities," he says. And it works. . . .

"You're dreaming up things all the time," said Julie Adler, one of the senator's chief press aides in the state. "You try to get the offbeat stuff."[12]

What Gets Through?

It would be foolish to argue that the media in general and television in particular have no effect on the selection of political candidates, their styles of political campaigning, and the outcome of elections—as foolish as saying that television "elected" Kennedy in 1960 or Nixon in 1968 or 1972. Clearly, there are an enormous number of variables involved. On one side, quite tangibly, are the millions of television viewers watching the news and being exposed to spot appeals. Television can put a Watergate on the map and inflate a politician's "recognition factor," making him or her a household name—at least in the eyes of other politicians. Television can also help "set the agenda" of issues in a political campaign, as a number of social science studies have demonstrated. Television may also have long-term, cumulative effects on voting decisions; some political advertising (free or controlled) may strengthen the resolve of the already committed voter, just as people who already own Dodge automobiles tend to read or watch the ads extolling the advantages of owning Dodges. Other appeals may influence the undecideds.

Yet for all of television's reach, who can say with certainty what gets through to the viewer? The most responsible social scientists—such as Ithiel Pool at MIT, Morris Janowitz at Chicago, Joseph Klapper at CBS—acknowledge that it still is outside the capacity of social research, even with the most elaborate field techniques available, to give a clear answer to the question of how news and information formats affect public attitudes and political decisions.[13] Mass communications seldom produce changes in a pure, consistently predictable way. Also, the viewer-voter represents an enormous variable, each man or women bringing his or her own screen to events. As the sociologist Bernard Berelson once observed, on any single subject, many may "hear" but few may "listen."

In the 1972 presidential campaign, for all the skill and money that went into advertising and media events, many may have heard, but who was listening? "Never has so much been spent to say so little to so many," Stanley Tannenbaum of the Kenyon and Eckhardt advertising agency declared on election eve, 1972. Over the last four months, Tannenbaum noted, the polls had registered very little change in voter preference. "If I had as little effect with $10 million of my client's money, I'd shoot myself. After all that advertising, they haven't moved the needle. . . ."[14]

The image makers didn't take Tannenbaum's dramatic advice. Two years later, in the congressional and governors' races of 1974, they were back, resilient as ever, with a fresh doctrine for achieving effectiveness. The contemporary 1974 style of political advertising moved away from slickness. Instead, the ads featured one homey face-to-the-camera asking for the viewer's vote. It was the old, scorned talking-head style of the 1950s—so old that it looked new. Political television had come full circle, back to its first tentative experiments.

In a sense, this is not bad news. There is now an opportunity for other fresh starts. Like the generals who are said to fight the next war with the weapons of the last war, journalists tend to cover, in the next political campaign, the issues of the last campaign. In the 1974 elections there was a great deal of discussion of campaign financing, which, a politician friend of mine says, was actually the story of the 1972 campaign. But in 1972, most journalists were CREEPing around the subject of money; instead, the press expended a lot of time on the so-called "moral issues"—which were the 1968 story.

Clearly, however, the part played by political television—whether free or controlled—still has not been adequately charted. As political advertising has gone back to square one in its assumptions, so too can political research return to basic principles of voter attention, media influence, and the still poorly understood interactions between the two.

SOURCES AND NOTES

I have relied on three major sources of information in this study: first, my own interviews, reporting, and research; second, the interviews, reporting, and research conducted by members of the News Study Group at MIT under my supervision; third, a variety of books, articles, monographs, research reports, memoranda, newspaper accounts, broadcast transcripts, and congressional hearings and reports. In all cases, responsibility for the analysis and interpretation of this material is my own. The specific sources follow.

Chapter 1
1. "The Harris Survey," copyright by the *Chicago Tribune*. See surveys from April 30, 1973, through June 28, 1973, particularly the survey for release Tuesday, May 8.
2. Newton Minow et al., *Presidential Television* (New York: Basic Books, 1973).
3. Michael J. Robinson and Philip M. Burgess, "The Edward M. Kennedy Speech: The Impact of a Prime-Time Television Appeal," *Television Quarterly*, Winter 1970, pp. 29–39.
4. Roland Cole, *Campaign Expenditures in Senate Elections*, unpublished Ph.D. thesis, Harvard University, 1975.

Chapter 2
1. For more detailed statistics on the television audience, consult the Television Information Office, 745 Fifth Avenue, New York, N.Y. 10022. Also see Leo Bogart, *The Age of Television* (New York: Ungar, 1970).
2. The materials on the Minneapolis–St. Paul studies are from Robert T. Bower, *Television and the Public* (New York: Holt, Rinehart & Winston, 1973).

3. Robert MacNeil, *The People Machine* (New York: Harper & Row, 1968). The critic Ben Bagdikian makes a similar point in his study *The Information Machines* (New York: Harper & Row, 1971).

4. The material on audience flow is based on my own interviews with Paul Klein and on Klein's article "The Men Who Run TV Aren't That Stupid . . . They Know Us Better Than You Think," *New York* magazine, January 25, 1971, p. 20.

5. Norman Mailer, *St. George and the God Father* (New York: New American Library, 1973).

6. For the best history of the early days of television, see Erik Barnouw, *The Image Empire* (New York: Oxford University Press, 1970). This is the third volume in his three-volume history of broadcasting in the United States. For an evocative account of the "Murrow Years" at CBS News, see Fred Friendly, *Due to Circumstances Beyond Our Control . . .* (New York: Random House, 1967).

7. For the complete list of television's biggest spenders, consult Broadcast Advertisers Reports, Inc.

Chapter 3

1. *Submission of Recorded Presidential Conversations to the Committee of the Judiciary of the House of Representatives by President Richard Nixon* (Washington: U.S. Government Printing Office, 1974). This is the heavily edited Nixon version of the White House tapes.

2. An account of the News Study Group's work on the Watergate hearings appeared as "The Folks in the Boondocks: Challenging a Journalistic Myth," Edwin Diamond, *Columbia Journalism Review*, November–December 1973, p. 58.

3. High Sidey of *Time* magazine recounted the conversation to me.

4. Bernard R. Berelson, Paul F. Lazarsfeld, and William N. McPhee, *Voting* (Chicago: University of Chicago Press, 1954). See also Paul F. Lazarsfeld, Bernard Berelson, and Hazel Gaudet, *The People's Choice* (New York: Columbia University Press, 1968).

5. See both Paul Cowan, *State Secrets* (New York: Holt, Rinehart & Winston, 1974) and Penn Kimball, *The Disconnected* (New York: Columbia University Press, 1974).

6. Gail Sheehy, "Watching Watergate in Archie Bunker Country," *New York* magazine, June 18, 1973, p. 35.

7. Scott Ward's studies for the Marketing Science Institute, a non-profit research center associated with Harvard Business School, are important reading. See, for example, his draft monograph "What Research Says About a Proposed Code on Television Advertising for Children."

8. Amitai Etzioni, "Nixon By a Landslide? No, By a Yawn," *Newsday*, November 9, 1972, p. 61.

Chapter 4

1. *The Politics of Broadcasting: du Pont-Columbia Survey of Broadcast Journalism 1971–72*, edited by Marvin Barrett (New York: Crowell, 1973).

2. The ABC News figures, as well as the figures for the other networks, come from ABC News Department of Research and Development, Harvey N. Gersin, director, March 9, 1973.

3. Andrew Stern's study, underwritten by the National Association of Broadcasters, was presented to the Radio Television News Directors Association annual meeting in Boston, September 29, 1971. Stern also discussed his work with the News Study Group at MIT.

4. John S. Saloma III and Frederick H. Sontag, *Parties* (New York: Knopf, 1972), p. 253.

5. The quotations from John Chancellor, Richard Wald, and the others quoted in this section come from my own interviews with them.

Chapter 5

1. Valuable annual surveys of broadcast journalism appear in the mid-August issues of *Broadcasting* magazine. The weekly *Broadcasting* and the weekly *Variety* are the best ways to stay informed about television developments.

2. Edward Barrett, "Folksy TV News," *Columbia Journalism Review*, November–December 1973, p. 16.

3. The statements of Richard Salant and the others quoted in this section come from my own interviews. For more on the

consultants, see Edwin Diamond, "TV News: Games Consultants Play," *Boston Phoenix*, September 17, 1974.

4. Another consultant, Alfred Gruber of Brand, Gruber, Stander & Co., has a somewhat different view of what viewers say they want in political reporting.   As Gruber told *Broadcasting* magazine (August 20, 1973), "There is strong evidence that people want the newscaster to tell them what the issues are, what they mean and even how to vote. We found that unbiased coverage of political events is as confusing to the viewer as the event itself."

5. Richard Townley, "The News Merchants," Parts I and II, *TV Guide*, March 9 and 14, 1974.

6. Ron Powers and Jerrold Oppenheim, "Is TV Too Profitable?" *Columbia Journalism Review*, May–June 1972, p. 7.

Chapter 6

1. Gloria Emerson gave a long and important interview to Debora Dehoyos of the News Study Group in March 1973.

2. For a solid account of the North Vietnamese–National Liberation Front offensive, see Don Oberdorfer, *Tet* (New York: Doubleday, 1971).

3. Apple's comments are from an interview with Jane Pratt.

4. Richard Dudman's articles, which first appeared in the *St. Louis Post-Dispatch*, were later published as *40 Days with the Enemy* (New York: Liveright, 1971).

5. Wassily Leontief, "Sails and Rudders, Ship of State," *New York Times*, March 16, 1973, p. 41.

6. The citations from *Time* and *Newsweek* can be found in "Vietnam: What Lessons?" a special issue of the *Columbia Journalism Review*, Winter 1970–1971. See particularly the excellent account of the *Maddox* and *C. Turner Joy* episodes by Don Stillman, p. 21.

7. The Av Westin memo is quoted in Edward Jay Epstein, *News from Nowhere* (New York: Random House, 1973), p. 17.

8. The James McCartney citations are from "Vietnam: What Lessons?" p. 53.

Chapter 7

1. The quotations from the journalists and editors in this chapter come from my own interviews with the individuals quoted. See also articles by James F. Hogue, Jr., and Edwin Diamond, "Lessons of the Pentagon Papers," *The Bulletin of the American Society of Newspaper Editors*, September 1971.

2. A good behind-the-scenes account of the energy and planning that went into the *Times* series can be found in the "Press" section of *Time* magazine, June 28, 1971, p. 45. See also *Times Talk*, the house organ of the New York Times Company, June 1971.

3. Sanford Ungar, *The Papers and the Papers* (New York: Dutton, 1972).

4. A. M. Rosenthal quoted by Sanford Ungar.

5. The Robert J. Samuelson materials are quoted in Steve Knoll, "When TV Was Offered the Pentagon Papers," *Columbia Journalism Review*, March–April 1972, p. 46.

Chapter 8

1. Otto Kerner et al., *Report of the National Advisory Commission on Civil Disorders* (New York: Bantam Books, 1968).

2. Jean Fairfax,"Contributing to Black Rage," *New York Times* July 26, 1970, Section 2, p. 15.

3. Since the early 1960s, regular reports on the appearances of blacks on television have been issued, first by Plotkin and Pugh for the New York Society for Ethical Culture (1962, 1964) and later by Plotkin for the NAACP Legal Defense Fund.

4. The employment figures for all minorities—women as well as blacks and other minority groups—have been steadily improving, according to the FCC. The Commission's figures, as reported in *Variety*, March 12, 1975, show that total employment by broadcasters with five or more on the payroll jumped from 136,960 in 1973 to 141,700 last year, a 3.5 percent rise. That was down from a 5 percent jump the previous year. The agency said that some 35,765 women were employed in 1974, about 25.2 percent of the total, up from 33,001 or 24 percent in 1973. Minority group employment, including Negro, Oriental, American Indian, and Spanish-surnamed Americans, accounted for 12.3 percent of the total

last year (1974), compared with 11.7 percent in 1973 and 10.6 percent for 1972. Blacks, the largest minority group, increased from 10,296 in 1973 to 11,188 in 1974, or 7.8 percent of the total, compared with 7.5 percent in 1973. Spanish-surnamed Americans comprised 3.3 percent of the total last year, up slightly from 3.1 percent in 1973 and 3 percent in 1972.

5. For another reminder of the heady atmosphere of the "Cable Fable" days, see Phyl Garland, "Blacks Challenge the Airwaves," *Ebony* magazine, November 1970, especially the statements by Tony Brown and Bill Wright.

Chapter 9

1. The quotations from Bonnie Angelo, as well as from the other reporters, come from my own interviews, unless otherwise noted.

2. Theodore White, *The Making of the President, 1972* (New York: Atheneum, 1973).

3. *Washington Post*, November 20, 1973, Style section, p. 1. The interview was done by Jean White of the *Post*.

4. Brit Hume, "Jack Anderson and the Eagleton Case," *Washington Monthly*, July–August 1974.

5. The quotations from Ford Rowan, Saul Pett, and Dr. Lester Grinspoon and from the other sources cited in this section come from my own interviews, unless otherwise noted.

6. James David Barber, *Presidential Character* (Englewood Cliffs, N.J.: Prentice-Hall, 1972), and Bruce Mazlish, *In Search of Nixon* (New York: Basic Books, 1973).

Chapter 10

1. Bob Woodward and Carl Bernstein, *All the President's Men* (New York: Simon & Schuster, 1973), p. 281.

2. For a good account of how the media handled the White House tapes, see *Editor and Publisher*, May 4, 1974, p. 9, and *Broadcasting* magazine, May 6, 1974, p. 37.

3. All citations are from the edited Nixon version of the White House tapes. The Nixon punctuation is followed.

4. "TRB Comments," *Boston Globe*, May 14, 1974. p. 23.

        Apple, Introduction to *The White House Transcripts*

        'k: Bantam, 1974).

6. Professor Walter Dean Burnham of MIT was particularly helpful in his discussions with me about the office of the presidency.

7. The "big city mayor" and the other sources quoted in this section are all from my own interviews, unless otherwise noted.

Chapter 11

1. The analysis of the "phases" of the Watergate coverage is based on interviews with Ben Bradlee of the *Washington Post*.

2. The fact that the News Study Group examined the *total* communications is important. The writer Edith Ephron undertook a hatchet job on the national television networks for their 1968 presidential campaign coverage; to take just one example of the slipshod methods in her book *The News Twisters*, she recorded the words of the broadcasts without reference to the accompanying pictures.

3. Dan Rather, "Watergate on TV," *Newsday*, December 16, 1973, Ideas section, p. 1.

4. Michael Robinson, "The Impact of Televised Hearings on Public Opinion," *Journal of Communication*, Spring 1974, pp. 17-30.

5. Kevin Phillips and Albert Sindlinger, *The Media Report*, Vol. 1, No. 4 (April 26, 1974).

6. Michael Ross, *Resistance to Racial Change in the Urban North: 1962-1968*, unpublished Ph.D. thesis, Harvard University, 1973. Professor Ross, now at Boston University, discussed his work with me.

Chapter 12

1. The Lindsay commercial is one of the political "documents" that the News Study Group has been collecting in recent years for study and analysis. It is a model of "informality"—the mayor is pictured in an open shirt with traffic sounds in the background. The "informality" was achieved, it is said, after no fewer than 27 "takes" of the commerical. David Garth, the political consultant, believes the commercial won the reelection for Lindsay.

2. Jim Callaway, *Politeia*, Vol. 1, No. 4 (Summer 1972), p. 36.

3. William Kloepfer, Jr., of the Tobacco Institute, the cigarette industry's trade association based in Washington, D.C., supplied the statistics and some of the interpretations for this section on smoking and the media.

4. The estimate of how much money is needed to run for governor of New York State comes from associates of Nelson Rockefeller, who ran successfully four times.

5. Herbert Alexander, "Broadcasting and Politics," in *The Electoral Process*, edited by M. Jennings and H. Zeigler (Englewood Cliffs, N.J.: Prentice-Hall, 1966), p. 81.

6. For an account of John Kennedy's use of polling techniques and other aspects of the "new politics," see Ithiel de Sola Pool and Robert Abelson, "The Simulmatics Project," *The Public Opinion Quarterly*, Vol. XXV, No. 2 (Summer 1961), pp. 167–183, and Ithiel de Sola Pool, Robert P. Abelson, and Samuel L. Popkin, *Candidates, Issues, and Strategies: A Computer Simulation of the 1960 and 1964 Presidential Elections* (Cambridge, Mass.: MIT Press, 1965).

7. Vic Fingerhut in the *Public Interest*, Fall 1971 issue, argued that the Nixon "media blitz" helped Hubert Humphrey since it called to the attention of the poor, less-educated Democratic voters the fact that there *was* an election going on.

8. Marquis Childs is quoted in *du Pont-Columbia Survey of Broadcast Journalism 1969–70*, edited by Marvin Barrett (New York: Grosset & Dunlap, 1970), p. 61.

9. "Value for Money?" *The Economist*, November 14, 1970, p. 50.

10. The material from Campaign Planners, Inc., comes from interviews with Barry Nova and from his article "The Night Humphrey Dozed Off and Other True Adventures of a Media Manipulator in Politics," *New York* magazine, June 19, 1972.

11. The "new politics" conference papers were collected into a handbook, *The Political Image Merchants*, edited by Ray Hiebert et al. (Washington: Acropolis, 1971).

12. Thomas Collins, *Newsday*, June 14, 1972, p. 15A.

13. For more on what is sent and what is received, see Wilbur ⸜ramm, "Channels and Audiences," in the *Handbook of Com-ˈcatons*, edited by I. de Sola Pool, F. Frey, W. Schramm, N. ⸜by, and E. Parker (Chicago: Rand McNally, 1970). ⸜nley Tannenbaum was interviewed by Philip H. Dougherty ⸜dvertising news column in the *New York Times*, November

INDEX

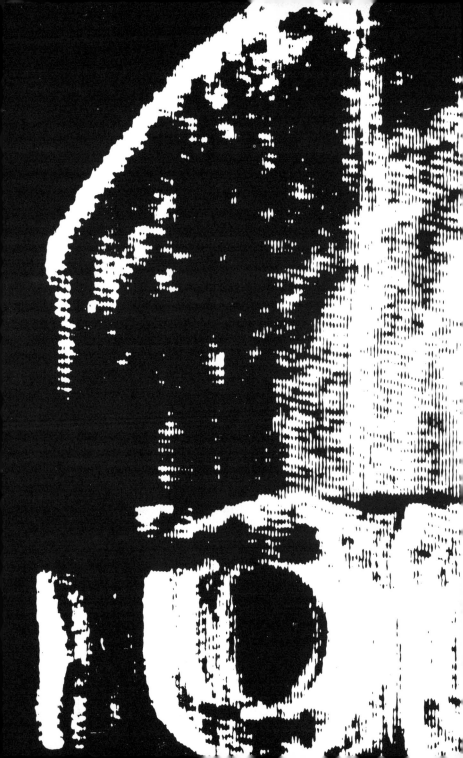

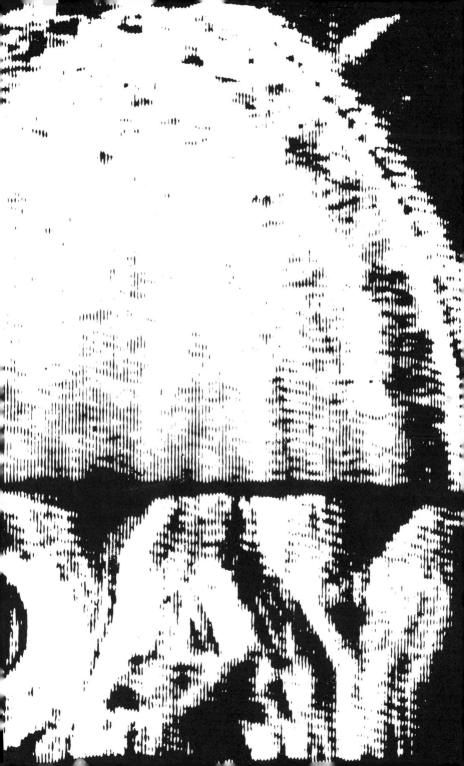